CW00746991

Published

Mereo is an imprint of Memoirs Publishing

25 Market Place, Cirencester, Gloucestershire, GL7 2NX
info@memoirsbooks.co.uk www.memoirspublishing.com

Diary of a village boy
The memoirs of an ordinary man and the times he lived through

All Rights Reserved. Copyright © 2013 Kevin James

ISBN: 978-1-909544-95-6

DIARY
OF A
Village Boy

The memoirs of an ordinary man and
the times he lived through

KEVIN JAMES

DIARY
OF A
Village Boy

The memoirs of an ordinary man and
the times he lived through

MEREO
Cirencester

PREFACE

From the early days of my life brought up in an opulent village, I was determined to study. At work I had tunnel vision, and work took priority over my personal life. This resulted in me leading more or less a single life. But I was proud of my work and the men who worked for us, and tried to treat them as friends.

This book tells of many incidents, some mischievous, some alcohol-related and some more everyday. I have written it to talk about my many memories.

INTRODUCTION

The following is a kind of life story, from the 1950s to the present day. Back in the early days my parents' marriage was not the most amicable, but I was too young to appreciate their circumstances. As we didn't have a smooth passage on our way to adulthood I recalled orchestrated and spontaneous events that occurred thought the years with a record in the charts that seemed to relate to it.

As a boy being brought up in a rather opulent village, Brent Knoll in Somerset, I was always out and about doing chores to earn a little cash, which gave me some ambitions to better myself, so telling this account of the more serious side of my nature I included these events that off set this rather personal struggle. I have no excuse for some of the things I did, futile as they may seem. As a lyric said in one song "I was just a boy…"

My father came from Ireland in the late 1940s, described in his passport as a professional rabbit catcher. In those days he worked with the pick and shovel and would have been regarded as an Irish navvy, but he was quite well read. He travelled from different sites until he met my mother, when he took up lodgings. My mother was the only child of a farm labourer. They married in 1950 and over the next seven years had five children, John, me, Michael, Rita and Patrick.

Summer days spent in a haze in woods we ran amongst the flowers
Bluebells, primrose we would spend hours
We played in hay lofts, picked apples too,
Played in fields the farmer knew.
We picked blackberries, nuts and even pears,
Collected conkers, we had no cares.
Harvest home came and went,
Pocket money was all spent.
Summer over, back to school,
Working hard was the rule.
When days turned cold with frost and snow,
Up the hill we would go
Home-made sledge and lots of kids,
Lots of crashes with bin lids.
Our house was cold and times were tough
We had each other, that was enough.
Summer, winter, we were young,
It didn't matter, it was fun.

1952-1955

When I came along, the second eldest, Mum and Dad had a chance to move out of their squalid cottage into a new council house, which had no central heating. There were coal fires upstairs and down, a toilet outside and a large garden. Our village might have had an aura of wealth about it, but we were most definitely poor.

Obviously I can't remember a lot of what was going on at this time, but up to when I was five I can vaguely remember the light blue cot I slept in and the high chair I was seated in. So I can remember from about five years old onwards, which was around 1957.

By late 1953 my brother was on the way. Television was catching on and the music scene was on the verge of changing from big band music to rock and roll.

Some of the headlines for 1952-55:

1952

King George VI dies, Princess
Elizabeth to be new Queen

Eva Peron dies

Flood devastates Devon village

Landslide victory for Eisenhower

Queen makes her first Christmas speech.

1953

Derek Bentley hanged for murder of policeman

Queen Mary dies peacefully

Hillary and Tenzing conquer Everest

Queen Elizabeth takes Coronation oath

John Christie hanged for serial murders

1954

Roger Bannister breaks the four-minute mile

Winston Churchill celebrates 80th birthday

End of rationing

US tests hydrogen bomb in Bikini Atoll

1955

Albert Einstein dies

Ruth Ellis hanged for killing lover

James Dean killed in car smash

Gaitskell elected Labour Leader

ITV ends BBC television monopoly

1956

As a four-year-old I can remember little things such as staring through the mesh at the chickens the neighbours kept, playing in the grass and being seated up in my high chair. Also picking currants (I didn't like them) from the cakes and watching my Dad drinking cider with a neighbour. The neighbour
would pass sweets through the garden gate. Our neighbour had a soft-spoken voice and was very kind, and her daughter would babysit. I also remember trying to play with their cats.

Some of the events that were in the news:
Hungarians rise up against Soviet rule
Allied forces take control of Suez
Prince Rainier marries Grace Kelly
Cambridge spies surface in Moscow.

The songs that were popular that year include *All Shook Up*, *Why Do Fools Fall in Love* and *Whatever Will Be Will Be*.

1957

This was the year I started school. I held on to the railings outside for dear life, and it took a lot of persuasion to get me in. All my clothes were hand-me-downs or from jumble sales. As the winter wore on, the teacher gave me a woollen balaclava head gear and mittens. In those days a 1/3 pint of milk was by the stove.

I can recall my nan approaching on her bike. This got us excited, as she would always have something to give us. My eczema started developing, along with asthma, which led to having coughs that went on for weeks due to the damp rooms. From now at least until I was 16 years old I had to battle this, which made me feel inferior. I had no confidence and was quite withdrawn, which resulted in me wanting to be successful.

World events of 1957:

Resignation of Sir Anthony Eden over Suez

Macmillan becomes Prime Minister

Britain drops its first H-Bomb

Sputnik satellite blasts into space, and dog becomes first 'astronaut'

Malaysia and Ghana celebrate independence

Rock and Roll hit the headlines after hits like *Garden of Eden* and *Singing the Blues*, then along came *All Shook Up* by Elvis Presley and *That'll Be the Day* by Buddy Holly. There was skiffle music from Lonny Donegan.

1958

I was now six years old and very aware that money was scarce, especially when we were told to hide under the table and keep quiet because the rent man was coming down the path and about to tap on the door.

My father used to drink cider. I recall being given a half of cider and falling out of the chair on to the cider jar and cutting my face above my eye. It bled profusely.

At six years old I was allowed to go to the shops up the road to buy some broken biscuits or four chews for a penny. My father would take us out blackberrying across the fields and we would then catch a bus into Burnham on Sea with our mum. Our playground was often the lane outside the house, which was a godsend because even at six years old I knew Mum and Dad were arguing over money and I was best out of the way.

Some of the events of 1958:

Manchester United players killed in
Munich air disaster

My Fair Lady dazzles London

Castro's rebels edge closer to Cuban capital

Explorer Sir Edmund Hillary arrives at South Pole.

The hit songs at this time included *All I Have to Do is Dream, When, All in the Game and It's Only Make Believe.*

1959

Periodically we would pay a visit to the hairdressers in a town a few miles away in a little side street, a place called Rawlinsons. My brother and I would probably have a basic cut, a sort of old fashioned short back and sides. Then we would go to the pub opposite the old railway terminus that used to be near the sea front.

I was now a shy freckle-faced kid with constant asthmatic problems, which led to me feeling inferior to others, but quite determined to succeed at what I did. I remember wearing Clarks' shoes, usually with holes in them, grey ankle socks, short trousers and a grey flannel shirt. I recall being allowed in the woods nearby and picking primroses, bluebells and violets and walking up the road to my Nan's. We would pass the Village Hall with rock and roll sounds echoing out of the windows.

Through the winter we prayed for snow because we had a great landscape around for sledging. During the summer we played in the fields of long grass doing hide and seek. We really got excited when we went to bed, quite early, to hear the ice cream van come down our lane. If our luck was in we would have one. At school you would hope there would be some absenteeism so there would be come milk left over, as the milk at home was like liquid gold and had to last.

We now had a small television set at home, and I remember the wrestling, *Robin Hood* and *Wagon Train*. The trouble was that the picture would go fuzzy and slip up and down. It was all operated by knobs - none of this remote control, even to make a phone call you had to go the phone box and press the A and B buttons.

Around this time my grandfather had a lodger, as this helped financially. From what we were told he was a reserved sort of character. One morning my grandfather got up, went into the kitchen and found the lodger with his head in the gas oven.

When the police came round they glared at my grandfather and asked him why he had moved the body. "Well, I had to cook my breakfast didn't I?" he replied. He was a man of simple values. Nothing was too serious for him, but obviously it was different for the lodger.

Some of the events of the time were:

De Gaulle becomes French President

Buddy Holly killed in air crash

Macmillan and Khruschev talk peace

Hovercraft marks a new era in transport

UK's first trunk call from a pay phone

Soviets launch rocket to the moon.

Hit songs at this time included *It Doesn't Matter Any More, Dream Lover, Living Doll, Here Comes the Summer, What Do You Want To Make Those Eyes At Me For* and *Mack the Knife*.

1960

On a typical day back then I would be suffering from asthma brought on by dampness and my chest would be congested. They decided I should visit the local clinic for physio on Tuesdays and Fridays. There I would be slapped about for half an hour.

On a few occasions my dad would be off work and he would take me to a pub in town. As you walked in you could smell the cider. All the blokes in there were studying the racing pages. They were all shapes and sizes, some wearing hats, some smoking heavily. Though most of them were in their late fifties, they looked older by today's standards.

I recall looking at the names of the horses, which helped me to relax and improved my breathing, but I was now hooked. I remember my first winner, whose name was Christmas Review. Horse racing was the only thing that seemed to help my breathing, as it had a calming influence on me.

In the evening I would walk to my elder brother's place (he lived with our grandparents). As I came down the street I would hear *Apache*, the Shadows' number 1 hit. We would then go collecting rubbish for the bonfire we were building for Guy Fawkes day. In those days the back of my nan's place had fields and often in the afternoon we would look through the mesh at the cows getting ready for milking.

A couple of funny events I can recall were our chimney catching fire and waking up next morning and finding cattle in the garden because someone had left a field gate open.

I acquired a tricycle, which kept me amused up and down the lane beside the house.

Events of the year included:

Scores die in Sharpeville shoot out, South Africa

Princess Margaret weds Anthony Armstrong Jones

Khrushchev anger erupts at UN

Narrow election victory for John F Kennedy

Lady Chatterley's Lover sells out after court case.

Records at this time seem to relate to some of the above mentioned. They included *Poor Me, Shaking All Over, Good Timing, Three Steps to Heaven* and *Starry Eyed.*

1961

I was now nine years old now and having a continual battle with asthma. I was in and out of the sanatorium in Weston Super Mare, eight miles away; my mother took me in on the bus. I used to fear the months of September to March, because most of the time I didn't sleep and sometimes had weeks off school. It set me back in learning at school. The trouble was that when I got back I was far behind and used to feel lost, so I didn't want to go back.

I used to go to the shops for neighbours and do odd jobs to earn a little pocket money, while I saved up for the village jumble sale, hoping to get some clothes. This would be on a Saturday afternoon. It was usually three old pence to get in and there was usually a stampede to get in when the doors opened at 2.30 pm.

We started to explore the village and go a bit further afield. We used to play a game called 'Release me'. One evening while getting over a fence I fell and fractured my arm, which put me in plaster for weeks.

There were a few kids in the family down our lane who I used to mix with and we would play around the barns in the field around the corner from us, but only when the farmer was out of sight.

There were also the celebrations for the centenary of the village school. We had a sports day and our photos were taken. One funny event, though also quite serious, was when Dad, slightly intoxicated, tried to help me make a rabbit hutch. He severed the top off his finger and a neighbour had to rush him to hospital.

Some of the events of this year were:

John F Kennedy sworn in as US President

Ukulele King George Formby dies

Berlin wakes to find the city divided

Couple found shot dead in A6 layby

Victorious Castro wins election

Shapford becomes first US astronaut

World watches Russian nuclear test

At the end of this year the birth control pill became available to all. The music of the time was about to be swamped within a couple of years by the Mersey Sound.

Hit songs of the year included *Tower of Strength, Wooden Heart, Walking Back to Happiness, Runaway, You Don't Know* and *Well I Ask You.*

1962

Life at home wasn't that good as there was nearly always a dispute, often leading to very heated moments which frightened us, so we were happier when we went out. Back then we had to earn our pocket money, and I did gardening during the summer for a retired Naval Commander. In the winter I used to sort out his fuel, which was had to be chopped up in three sizes. I worked for this particular couple on Saturday and Sunday mornings for the next eight or nine years.

I would go blackberrying with my five-year-old brother Patrick from about 7.30 am to 5 pm, sometimes coming back dinner time. We would save up all the blackberries for Saturday morning when Joe and his van would turn up to weigh them. Of course a few jugs of water over them the night before would help make a better deal. He would pay us sixpence a pound. Looking back, we never had to worry about strangers considering we were on our own all day.

In my last year at primary school, I remember realising that we all seemed destined to go to the secondary modern school.

I loved rounders. One day some soiled underwear

was found in the field while we were playing. Of course there was an inspection to find the culprit, and when eventually one pupil was discovered without his pants on his excuse was that he had forgotten to wear them.

Like most of us pupils I eventually had to do a hundred lines, in my case for swearing at a girl pupil.

On wet days when it was difficult to earn money, we would go to a house on the hill which was surrounded by woods and be given a ball of coloured wool. We would strip the ivy off the trees and then tie wool round to identify it as one that had been stripped. We would also look in hedgerows for empty lemonade bottles and hand them in to the shops for cash – you got threepence or so back on bottles in those days.

Sometimes the lady whose trees we stripped would have us collecting any dead wood and taking them down into the yard for sawing.

Some events that year:

A6 murder trial – Hanratty hanged for murder

Russia frees US spy plane pilot

Three escape Alcatraz

Marilyn Munroe found dead

Mississippi race riots over first black student

World relief as Cuban missile crisis ends

Choking fogs spread across Britain.

The music that seems apt for this time included *Come Outside, Telstar, Wonderful Land, Return to Sender, Good Luck Charm* and *The Young Ones.*

1963

Towards the end of this year I started secondary modern school, which I found, as a quiet village boy, quite overwhelming. It was a long day. We caught the school coach at 8.15 am, as the school was seven miles away in Weston Super Mare.

There was quite a strict regime. At least if we were a bit scruffy we weren't alone, as in the previous village school you would stand out. We always looked forward to dinner times, when the tables were put together to form an octagon. You could guarantee we were nearly always last and looking for a second helping.

Some of my best memories are of times when the school coach couldn't pick me up due to the horrendous winter. We would scamper home and dress up well and go out sledging on an 8' x 4' sheet of galvanised corrugated iron with sharp edges folded over. The snowdrifts covered over ditches that separated fields. I recall walking over drifts and vanishing down into the hedge, but everything was so picturesque.

I was 10 years old and getting on for 11, and I now had quite a few gardening jobs around the village. I also had a bicycle and a home-made go-kart produced from some old pram wheels; we used to have races down the hill, oblivious to danger. We spent very little time at home. Our favourite times were when we were tucked up in a hayrick. We always knew when the farmer was coming as the sound of the John Deere tractor was a warning he was on the way.

We went to the local cinema 2-3 miles away to see Cliff Richard in *Summer Holiday*, then saved our money through the weeks to go down to town and treat ourselves to a meal before going to Woolworths for pick 'n' mix. The manager walked around as if he was in the Gestapo. I remember in particular his hairstyle, creamed and parted down the middle to look like a woodlouse. Then we would go to the amusement arcade and find ourselves having to walk home, skint.

1963 was infamous for its bitter winter. Our council house didn't have any heating apart from the coal fires, and the toilet was outside, so we kept a bucket on the landing. Our rooms were damp, and to keep warm I used old coats from the jumble sale and put them on top of the sheets. The trouble was the window would never shut correctly.

As the night progressed a blizzard raged. My window opened in the night and the snow came in and covered us six inches deep - that was our little taste of that dreadful winter. We slept quite well because of the cider we had drunk earlier. It looked quite scenic, the snow hanging off the chest of drawers and chairs – very ornate!

Some of the events of the year were:

Kennedy shot dead in Dallas, the assassin murdered,
Johnson takes over as president

Railway network to be slashed by a quarter

Profumo resigns over sex scandal

Train robbers make off with millions

Martin Luther King dreams of racial harmony

The invention of a train that drives itself.

Beatlemania took us by storm that year. Some of the music of the time was *From Me to You, She Loves You, I Want to Hold Your Hand, How Do You Do It, You'll Never Walk Alone, I Like It* and *Devil In Disguise.*

1964

Things at home weren't good as my father was now out of work. My mother took on cleaning jobs. We would find them most evenings arguing, usually about money. We built a shed so I could do my homework in peace, in the former chicken run. The priest intervened once to save us from eviction, but in turn we kids were expected to take up religion and cycle three miles behind our father to the church, then back afterwards while he went for refreshment. Luckily this ordeal didn't last long.

My father brought a lot of his way of life with him. Heavy smoking and sometimes drinking took over, but in his own way he did care for us.

One cold evening he became desperate for a Woodbine cigarette, and was cursing in his Irish accent, "A man hasn't even got the price for a fag". He seemed to be cutting up some papers to roll for cigarettes, and then seemed transfixed; something calmed him. We kids would watch as he approached the Brooke Bond tea packet and to our astonishment rolled himself some fags from the tea. When he went out we dived for the packet of tea, deciding it was a great idea. The three of us smoked ourselves silly. Next day we were sick and off school for four days, but the doctor never knew.

Of course, not having much money meant that even coal for the fire was a luxury. My father's skill as a professional rabbit catcher was put to use up in the surrounding hills and he showed us where the snares were. So in the mornings we had to go out at 5.30 am, taking our go-kart with us over the hill to collect all the dead wood we could and sort the rabbits out. It was nearly always frosty. We always hoped we wouldn't find the rabbits still alive in the snares. Then it was back down the hill with a loaded kart. Burning wood wasn't good for the chimney, as we were to learn later.

The main thing I remember is how picturesque everything was when frosty or snowy. On the way back home we used to get some strange looks as the go-kart was full of wood.

All that winter of 1963-4 we came home from school to a freezing house, which had no fire lit. My sister started to organise lighting a fire. I was getting changed and could see she was struggling. Then suddenly I had a brainwave. I remembered that there was a gallon of paraffin in the shed. I said to my sister, "Don't worry, problem solved, I've got the answer."

I came in with the paraffin and said "Step back, I'll get the fire going". Then I heaved the tin forward. There was an almighty flash, bang and roar and my hair and eyebrows were singed as well as the wallpaper. Outside the chimney-pot had blown off and flames were shooting in the air.

The neighbours were stunned. I could hear the fire engines in the distance, but at least we got the fire started!

Some of the events of that year were:

Beatlemania arrives in the USA

Cassius Clay crowned boxing World Champion

Nelson Mandela jailed for life

Train robbers get a total of 300 years in jail

The Sun newspaper is born

The Forth Road Bridge opens

Sir Donald Campbell speeds to a double record

President Johnson signs the civil rights bill.

Some of the music at this time: *House of the Rising Sun, Dance On, World Without Love, Can't Buy Me Love, Don't Throw Your Love Away, Have I The Right, It's Over, Needles and Pins* and finally *Always Something There to Remind Me.*

1965

Some of the events I recall were mischievous, bearing in mind we were at the age to look for excitement and were often bored, as we used to meet up in the evenings rather than go home, especially on the more wintry nights when we couldn't do our gardening jobs. Sometimes we would stick up skittle pins to earn a little. Often we would take a gallon of cider up over the hills and light a fire, and even try a cigarette brand called Consulate. Of course then there were hardly any police about in the unlit roads of the village. We each had our own gardening job, and we used to saw up dead wood for a lady who lived in the woods.

We were now old enough to use bow saws to cut wood ourselves. I have to say it was usually just two of us, me and John, on these mischievous pranks and we never set out to hurt anyone.

Some stories from that year:

The precious plant
On a mild windy day in spring a friend and I, both of us about 13 years old, took on a gardening job on for a

lady known as Mrs G, who furnished us with a swing king cutter, a sort of scythe. We were given a tour of where she wanted the grass cutting, and she stopped suddenly at one point to show us a particular plant, approximately five feet tall, which she emphasised was rare and had taken her years to nurture and treasure. She explained to us how precious it was and said we were to treat the grass carefully around the trunk. She then went out and left us to it.

When we had finished the job my mate cut the plant down by accident. By the time Mrs G got back we had propped the plant up with some splints. She came out with her purse to pay us, but as she opened it to get the money out a sudden breeze came along and down came the precious plant across her feet. She hit the roof and we had to clear off without any money. I remember the Moody Blues' *Go Now* playing at that time.

Scrumping - a bridge too far
One dusky summer's evening, a friend and I were helping ourselves to some apples, and larking about hiding behind trees and hurling them at each other. Suddenly in the distance at the end of the orchard a very irate farmer appeared, waving a large stick and shouting at the top of his voice. We fled to the end of the orchard, where we knew from blackberrying that there was a footbridge across the field. We got across but he wasn't far away, so we went like the clappers. He was still chasing us and shouting aloud.

We got across another footbridge and couldn't believe he was still chasing us. We knew of one more footbridge where we would have to cross the railway lines. The last bridge was fairly rotten in the middle and we skipped across and headed for the lines when he came across the bridge. It collapsed, sending him knee deep into the water and brambles. It was a great escape for us but unfortunately we lost the few apples we had. The grass is not always greener on the other side.

A present for you

On a cold murky day my mate and I were walking down the road when we came across some cardboard boxes and wrapping paper ready for the bin man. We thought up a naughty but hilarious trick. We took the items to a cow shed, where we proceeded to fill the two boxes with the animal produce from the cow shed. Then, carefully wrapping it very tastefully, we waited for evening to come. At about 9.30 we placed a package in the quiet, unlit road, then waited across the road where an old shed and two bush trees were.

We were standing in the trees waiting when all of a sudden a maroon Jaguar rolled up. Out of the back of the car a young lady excitedly jumped up into the road, took the box and put it in the back of the car.

By now we were almost crying with laughter, but worse was to come. She decided to open it up. After a fierce struggle it ripped open and the contents were scattered around the inside of the car. We were almost falling out of the trees. It wasn't pleasant, but it was certainly hilarious.

It didn't stop there. The local gossip came by on her bike. She stopped and picked up another parcel, and this went to lost property in the Post Office, or so we learned.

One too many throws

One evening during the winter my mother was watching a TV programme, Father was out and we were shut out in the kitchen area. My brother and I were bored, so we started throwing a ball about. When I threw it at him he was standing in front of the back door. He ducked the ball and it hit the crinkle-patterned glass, which cracked all over. We decided to head for bed.

Later that evening Dad came home from the pub and we could hear the gate slam. He was singing *When Irish Eyes Are Smiling*. When he got in he slammed the door in question, and as he did so the glass fell into his face. He came into our bedroom with blood dripping from his face, demanding an explanation. Next day with what money I had earned from gardening I went down to the local builder and got a new sheet of glass, but it did sober him up at the time.

By the end of this year I was fighting back at the asthma by getting up earlier in the morning and doing press ups on the lawn and practising running around the village.

Key news events:

Sir Winston Churchill dies

Thousands join Martin Luther King in Alabama Rally

Huge Rhodesia win for Ian Smith;
Rhodesia breaks from UK

Drink drive alcohol limit to be introduced

Edward Heath chosen as new Tory leader

50,000 troops sent to Vietnam

Ronald Biggs escapes jail

Indian army invades West Pakistan.

The hits of the time included: *Help, Get Off My Cloud, Tired of Waiting For You, Concrete and Clay, The Last Time, I Got You Babe, Make It Easy On Yourself, Tears, Mr Tambourine Man* and *King of the Road.*

1966

By now my mates and I were often pushing our luck with some of the pranks. Boredom was part of the problem. In the next two or three years we were close to going off the straight road into the world of criminality, and it was only some teachers and people I worked for on gardening jobs who eventually pushed us the right way. I suppose the old Commander I had worked for at weekends since I was about 10 years old had some influence on me - he was "old school".

I was now friendly with a chap on the school bus called Paul, whose father ran a restaurant. We got to be good friends because we studied the horse racing pages. He used to smuggle out booze of all sorts, put it in a bag in a dry ditch next to the farmers haystack, and we would go over later and get fairly stoned. The dodgy bit was trying to get home! We would often go back the short cut and come across geese which gave us a hard time.

On one occasion in this field we were tipsy and propelled mud across the hedge on to a large transport lorry which pulled up sharply. He came back down the road with a large club in his hand and a torch. We buried ourselves down in the ditch and prayed he didn't notice us. It was pitch dark and it certainly scared us.

Another event that year was breaking my other arm, after this rather naughty escape.

New shoes

At thirteen years old any money I got was from gardening or blackberrying, and we would use it to catch the bus into the town and treat ourselves to a meal, then go down the park. One afternoon I noticed a pair of boots described as an Italian fall boot, purple with silver chains and hooks for laces. They cost 30 shillings, beyond my reach, but I had never had a new pair of boots or shoes. I always had hand-me-downs or jumble sale ones.

One day we were in a field next door to the hall where the jumble sale was being held at and we noticed them bringing in the gear ready to sell the next day. We waited until nightfall, scaled the drainpipe and then got in through the small window and sorted some clothes out. We noticed the meter box had not been shut correctly and took out about 30 shillings each. The next day I went straight to the shoe shop and paid the 30 shilling pieces for the boots. The man jokingly replied "Anyone would think you've robbed a gas meter", to which I replied that that was how we got paid for blackberrying. I sat in the park and took my holey shoes off and stuck the new ones on, I felt great. But there was a sense of guilt as we had always earned our money.

Old Fred hits back

Sometimes being in the village could be a little boring, so we often looked for a bit of fun. A certain elderly gentleman dressed in old overalls and a flat hat and carrying a walking stick would travel down to the local pub at about 9.30-10 pm every night. On his route in the pitch dark of night he had to pass a 4ft high wall separating a field from the main village road, and as he was approaching this wall we would be hiding and shouting obscenities at him. One night he passed very quietly and then all of a sudden in the dark my mate took several wallops from his walking stick, but he missed me. He then went on his way coughing in the pitch dark to the pub, leaving my mate nursing his ear and cursing.

The Gigolo

One gloomy wet afternoon I was tidying up the back of the garden at a lady's house in the village. I went round to the back of the house earlier than expected and saw a man in a hat and a long overcoat running up the path, with the lady saying "F… off you gigolo!" I was totally struck dumb. She paid me and I went home to my mum and asked what a gigolo was. She said "Don't worry about that, just you concentrate on cutting the grass".

Some world events:

Indira Ghandi takes charge in India

Harold Wilson wins sweeping election victory

Moors murderers jailed for life

Football glory for England in the World Cup

Children die in slag heap collapse in Aberfan

Arrests in London after anti-Vietnam War rally

Vietcong bomb Saigon

BBC tunes into colour

Soviets land probe on the moon.

Some of the other music at this time was *Strangers in the Night, These Boots are made for Walking, Somebody Help Me, Good Vibrations Out of Time, Keep on Running, All Or Nothing, Pretty Flamingo, Yellow Submarine, Green Green Grass of Home, With a Girl Like You* and finally *You Don't Have to Say You Love Me.*

1967

The summer of love

This was the year when I had a crush on a girl call Inez but couldn't tell her. She was petite with tawny coloured skin. I had an instant attraction to her but lacked that confidence to try my luck. I was not quite 15 years old. I do wonder where she is now and what she is like.

I acquired a tandem bike, and my sister and I would tear round the village and my mate and I would cycle to skittle weekends in hope of winning the prizes. It was the year when the music was all about flower power in San Francisco and the euphoria it caused.

My father got a maintenance job at a holiday centre five or six miles away. He got me a job in the kitchen dining room helping a Cockney woman called Mavis, in her forties, who lived with a cigarette hanging out of her mouth all day. It was a great memory because of the holiday aura and the great records playing in the background, such as *San Francisco* and *All You Need is Love*, I was just a boy surrounded by some attractive female staff. It was great been fawned over.

Whiter shade of pale

During my school holidays I helped out in the dining area pushing a trolley round collecting dirty plates etc. The kitchen had some hot-headed foreign workers. Two blokes earlier on were having words about pretty Brigitte and who was going out with her. I used to finish at 2.30-3.30 pm, then go round to the workmen, but when my dad used to be stationed ready for call out I would drink their cider. It was very bitter but I wouldn't say that to them.

I also watched the horse racing. I loved the atmosphere at this time as it got me away from everyday life at home.

One particular day I walked into the kitchen with at least 30 plates in my hands to find an almighty slanging match taking place. The man beside me picked up a large knife and hurled it at the man opposite us by the exit door. It stuck in the door right by his ear, and scared the wits out of me. Understandably I dropped all the plates. I thought it was unreal, and as the record says I turned a whiter shade of pale. But I still looked forward to 2.30 pm as this was when I could choose a meal for nothing and have as much milk as I fancied.

Towards the latter park of the year we asked the farmer for his empty cow cake meal bags for a small business venture. We went up to the woods at night and early morning, got what dead wood was available and sawed down a few odd trees which we thought people wouldn't notice were missing. We covered the stumps with mud and grass. Sunday night while listening to *Pick of the Pops* we would saw up the logs and bag them, then sell them for two shillings a bag. Then we would go off to the hills and have a few beers. When we told the story to our mates at school, this led to another event.

A drop at school

That summer I was friendly with a lad called Paul whose father owned a restaurant-cum-club venue. We were quite used to obtaining cider on a dull day and sitting inside a hayrick and drinking it, sometimes until we were ill, but it was boredom that led us to do this. The cider was cheap and we obtained it from a local farm that brewed it.

On a winter's day we loved the smell of hay when we were tucked up in a hay rick away from everyone, especially if it was snowing. When night fell, we used to walk over to this restaurant and in a hedge alongside the road would be a bag filled up with assorted booze which we would take back to the hayrick and drink. One day I took a suitcase to school and during the lunch break I and four others slipped off to a dry ditch on the outskirts of the playing field and drank to our hearts' content. We took some strong mints to hide the smell.

When we got back to class, to our surprise we had a mock history exam. We sat there full of life until the booze took effect. We gaped at each other, totally perplexed. The teacher sensed something was wrong. Thank heavens for mints! The five of us got no further than writing our names down, the rest went blank. There was a bit of an inquisition, but I got away with it.

Some of the events that year were:

Sir Donald Campbell killed during speed
record attempt

Supertanker Torrey Canyon hits rock and spills oil

Sir Francis Chichester completes single-handed
voyage round the world

Israel ends six-day war

Beatles Manager Brian Epstein commits suicide

Cuban rebel leader Che Guevara shot dead

Thousands join anti-war movement

Foot and mouth disease slaughter rate soars

Stones guitarist Keith Richards escapes jail for drugs

Music at the time included *Silence is Golden, All You Need Is Love, Puppet on a String, San Francisco, The Last Waltz, Release Me, I'm a Believer, Massachusetts, Let the Heartache Begin* and *Sergeant Pepper's Lonely Hearts Club Band*, the classic Beatles album.

1968

In 1968 I was at the tail end of my secondary education. I took six GCEs, avoiding the music and art because of cost, which I regret. My parents were nearly always at loggerheads so always my studying was in the shed I had built. I felt I had to carry on and get an apprenticeship with a trade. I didn't want to be short of money, and I wanted to have some fun. I felt I was living a life of two personalities.

I finished school in May 1968 to the sound of a famous record in the charts, *Young Girl* by Union Gap. I managed to obtain an apprenticeship at an engineering factory about three miles away, to start in August, so in the meantime I went gardening and haymaking.

Don't play with knives
My brother Michael and I were 14-15 year olds with a lot of daredevilry about us. We were always firing pellet guns, making bow and arrows or playing stitch. We would usually have a knife each and throw the knife at the ground. One day we were arguing, and I told Michael that if he didn't let up I would throw the knife at him. He kept saying I wouldn't dare, so I threw it so as to just miss him. But he raised his arms up. The knife struck his elbow and blood spurted out.

The neighbour opposite was just about to hang her washing up on the line when she dropped it all in the mud due to fright. I often regret this.

The first cut is the deepest

In early July that year a friend of mine in the village, a rather eccentric Rolling Stones fan called Rodney, acquired a motor bike and sidecar and we used to go into town three miles away. One night I went dressed in blue and white striped jeans, zip up boots and black T-shirt. We met a few others in a coffee bar on the coast six miles away. That was it, I knew I loved motorbikes. It was a form of escapism.

On July 20 I was hoping to go down to the coffee bar but my friend couldn't make it. The next day while cutting the hedge for an old customer of mine, the Commander, I learned that one of the lads had died in an accident, which made my fathers words of dislike for motorbikes echo in my head.

While I was cutting the hedge that day, I saw opposite me cleaning his maroon Jaguar Dickie Henderson, the TV star, who was staying with relatives. I wasn't totally convinced it was him until I saw the number plate on his car. He just said good morning.

I started my apprenticeship, which involved working a few weeks at the factory and then a year of full-time technical college.

The hand of God

I used to cycle every day three miles to work in the

factory labouring, doing jobs such as picking up sheet metal, until I started technical college. One evening after work I was coming up the garden path when I saw the priest with my dad. I had just finished work and said I didn't want to know. My dad got enraged and picked up the broom and was gong to hit me over the head with it, when the priest stepped in and said "No need to go to that extreme, let him make his own mind up".

Some of the events of that year were:

Damages for thalidomide children

Martin Luther King shot dead - James Earl Ray quizzed over King's death

United States erupts into race violence

Formula One ace Jim Clark killed at Hockenheim

Decimal coins reach the high street

Surgeons conduct UK's first heart transplant

Manchester United win European cup

Birth of sextuplets stuns Britain

Nixon elected US president

Mary Bell found guilty of killing two children

Songs of that year were: *I've got to get a message to you, Everlasting Love, I Pretend, Congratulations, With a Little Help From My Friends, Fire, Hey Jude, What a Wonderful World, Those Were the Days, Mary Mary* and *The Good, the Bad and the Ugly.*

1969

In the latter part of this year I obtained my first motorbike, having learned up in the fields over the hill in a clandestine fashion. In the meantime I was still studying during my first year at college full time. I was fed up with the small allowance we got. That first year I had to cycle three miles, then catch a bus to college, and Fridays we didn't finish till 8 pm. Occasionally a friend who had a white 750cc Norton would come along and pick me up. It was five or six minutes of sheer speed. The flesh on my cheeks was pulling and I was hanging on for dear life with my briefcase - bear in mind I had no helmet.

Often I would hitch-hike back, just to save the bus fare allowance. Every night I would do the homework set as soon as I had my tea. I thought one day it might be useful. Until I got my first bike, I used to go pillion on my mate's bike, who was competent but bloody fast, but fear was not in my vocabulary then.

Sunday afternoon explosion
When I was tidying up the tennis club shed I discovered some weedkiller. I took some home and experimented

with aerosol cans and a cup of sugar. It proved to be quite explosive.

One Sunday afternoon a friend of mine and I set about cutting up an old bicycle frame (tubular) in my shed, where I also studied metalwork. I had a hacksaw and a vice fixed to a bench where we could cut up the frames. We folded one end of the tube, stuffed the mixture into the pipe with cotton wool, placed it in a vice and put a length of old scaffold tube over the end so as we stood outside we could lever round and bend the end over. But as we folded it there was an almighty explosion, and the shed roof was seen spinning up into the air. Leaves fell out of the trees and windows rattled and opened. It would probably have killed us if we had stayed in the shed, but the excitement to us young lads was great.

I had previously set off several of these explosions around the district and eventually someone reported me and the police surrounded the house. To cut a long story short I had to promise to keep this concoction to myself. After a meeting with a police sergeant I was very close to being sent away.

During this year at technical college I was treated like an outcast because I tried hard at college. I used to stay on my own where possible rather than have any bother. The trouble was, none of my school friends went to this college and to put it lightly some of the pupils were rough. But before the above-mentioned incident, some of the class came to watch me blowing up two old-fashioned sinks in a field. For some reason from then onwards they seemed a little more amicable. The trouble was that we were hooked on the excitement of these escapades. Once I came out of the cinema with a policeman standing outside with a shovel in his hand with a piece of molten metal on it. Of course it had to cease.

World events included:

Man walks on the moon

Concorde flies for the first time

Murdoch wins Fleet Street foothold

Kray twins found guilty of McVitie murder

Bernadette Devlin is youngest-ever woman MP

Film star Sharon Tate murdered in ritual killings

British troops sent to Northern Ireland

Shelter exposes slum homelessness

Lulu ties the knot with a Bee Gee

Paul McCartney marries Linda Eastman

Brian Jones of the Rolling Stones dies of
drink and drugs.

Ben Sherman shirts and Doc Marten boots were in fashion. Skinheads clashed with greasers, similar to the mods and rockers era. Music included *Heard it Through the Grapevine, Bad Man River, Something in the Air, Sugar Sugar, Get Back, If Paradise is Half as Nice* and *Albatross.*

1970

I was 17 going on 18 and beginning to feel my feet, but life at home wasn't good. All my homework from day release technical college I would do in the galvanised shed I had built. I still had my gardening customers to see to in the evenings, and the money I tried to save went towards my first motorbike. My father emphasised that no motorbikes were coming on our patch, so my neighbour let me put it next door until he relented.

Some evenings my friend Rodney and I would go into town with me as a pillion passenger. Of course some nights were lively with the disco scene, involving reggae and motown. The temptation of getting a labouring job with some more money and no studying was always there, but support and advice from the old couple I worked for at weekends kept me going.

I loved eyeing up the girls but lacked confidence, and at times money and transport, but later I did pass my test on a 125cc Honda. In my first venture on heading into town I came round a bend and shot up through the rows of traffic, damaging some of the vehicles. I lay low for a while. As I said previously, I had cycled to town three miles away to catch the bus to college, where I and my workmates would study all day until 8 pm. The trouble was you couldn't take one exam again as you had to take all four at the same time.

We had a break at midday and then straight to the pub for darts and ham rolls.

Stronger than I thought

I was doing my apprenticeship at a college in a different area to my school, so I hardly knew anyone. I was learning bending and folding metals. I was nicknamed Desperate Dan because of my thick curly hair. My teacher was a Lancashire man in his late fifties, who we called Tatlock after the Coronation Street character. He was watching me trying to lift the handlebars up to fold the metal when I gave it an almighty wrench and the bars and the fold in the machine came crashing to the floor. I came out and the machine bent over with me hanging on to it, crashing over the floor. He was in stitches, his eyes streaming. He said in all his years of teaching he had never experienced anything as hilarious.

World headlines:

Gaddafi takes over as Libyan premier

Ian Smith declares Rhodesia a republic

Ian Paisley victory rattles NI Parliament

Violence flares as Bernadette Devlin is arrested

England captain Bobby Moore cleared of stealing

Civil war breaks out in Jordan

Rock legend Jimi Hendrix dies after party
Arab leaders sign Jordan peace deal
Large oil field found in North Sea
France mourns death of De Gaulle
Golden girl of athletics Lillian Board dies
Heathrow welcomes first jumbo jet.

The music of the time included *Tears of a Clown, Bridge Over Troubled Water, Love Grows Where My Rosemary Goes, Spirit in the Sky, Yellow River, Band of Gold, In the Summer Time, Woodstock* and *The Wonder of You.*

1971

This was the year I acquired another Honda motorbike, 160 cc, which became my pride and joy. Every day after work and my evening job and any homework I had to do, I would tear off up to town practising my handling, showing off on a quiet country road and pushing my luck. One afternoon in town I ended up in a shoe shop doorway, and the customers of a fish-and-chip shop scattered their food in fright.

Then as I was going home from work one evening a big van pulled out in front of me. I hit it and the bike wedged under the van, which was partly across the road. They had to get the services to jack the van up to get the bike out and it held up all the traffic on the main road. Most people thought the motorcyclist must be lying dead or injured under the van. It was chaos but I wasn't hurt.

I just couldn't resist making a noise. I put steel studs in the heels of my zip-up boots. When riding out of a bend I would put my foot down and showers of sparks would appear - anything to get noticed. Often my sister would come on the back as pillion just to get away for a change.

I was now in a local skittle team and took a keen interest. I felt at this stage in my life that everything seemed to come back to money. The temptation was to pack up the apprenticeship, and I was close to getting on the wrong side of the law, but I always remembered what the house was like when we were skint, which made me determined to at least try and better myself even though it seemed I had two personalities on the go.

I was in my ninth year of looking after the couple when he died and his wife eventually was put in a home by her daughter, who had to leave Ceylon. She asked me round to see her and presented me with a coal scuttle with a hole in the bottom, saying that with my knowledge from college I should be able to fix it. Well that put me in my place.

Headlines:

Idi Amin becomes Ugandan president

Post strike ends in pay deal

Council defies Thatcher milk ban

Doors singer Jim Morrison found dead

British troops shoot Londonderry rioters

'V' sign costs rider Harvey Smith victory

Bomb explodes in Post Office Tower

Pakistan intensifies air raids in India

Bomb demolishes crowded Belfast pub

American probe orbits Mars

Seals shot by government decree.

Popular songs included *Chirpy Chirpy Cheep Cheep*, *My Sweet Lord*, *Get It On*, *Coz I Love You*, *Knock Three Times* and *Hey Girl Don't Bother Me*.

1972

1972 was my favourite year, with some sadness but mainly joy. It was the year I got the bike and the girl and moved to town.

Having passed my motorbike test, I was always looking out for a larger bike, but alas money got in the way. Eventually my neighbour decided to sell his 500cc Triumph for £50. It was a 1960 model with side panels and crash bars at the rear.

I wheeled the bike up outside the garden shed and proceeded to stamp my identity on it. I painted it black, then carefully painted a white diamond each side and white stripes down along the forks at the front. I put on 18" high handlebars, and finally fitted over the seat the lining of a leopardskin coat. My father looked on with disdain. I remember the record *Son of my Father* playing.

I stood back and admired my handiwork and thought this was the business. I just couldn't wait to make my impression on the town. I even made a waistcoat out of sheepskin with studs around the periphery, and I still have it today. I had to be different, so I suppose I attracted some attention, which certainly stirred my father up. He was muttering that would never be seen on that contraption as I flicked around touching it up with a cloth to make it shine.

When I started going to town I felt like a million dollars. I would do all the homework (which wasn't much, as we were on day release), then head into the pub, a popular pub for the bikers, and sit their drinking lagers, listening to sounds like *Metal Guru* and *Vincent*.

One night I took three girls down to a barbecue five miles away. At last I was the bee's knees. The following night I met up with Nina, the girl I had taken down last of all, and we struck up a relationship. In later years this turned into marriage.

I couldn't stand crash helmets or too much clobber, but always wore the zip-up boots, thick denim jeans, black T-shirts and occasionally black leather jackets. The one I had was known as a flying jacket. After courting I would head back to my home in the village three miles away. Regularly I would approach the roundabout practising my leaning-over skills, which often sent sparks flying due to the crash bars digging in or grazing the road. The police pursued me on a few occasions, mainly to just lecture me.

Sometimes when I arrived home I would have to scale the drainpipe to get in through my sister's bedroom window. My father was then quite awkward with me. Then one night I came home, and as usual he had a certain amount of alcohol in him and was cursing me. I was no longer going to be intimidated, and I stood my ground and answered back. I stood up to him and he came at me. I defended myself and knocked him down.

Ominously, he said I would pay a price for this, but through working and not sleeping I suffered from nervous exhaustion. Finally I went to live with my girlfriend. I could say I always regretted this but eventually six weeks later we settled our differences and became like mates.

Light my fire

I decided to visit my dad and brother one hot afternoon. I rode out with my girlfriend on my Triumph and on arrival my brother Michael was as usual trying to light a bonfire - he was always attracted to fire. We were in the kitchen chatting when he came in looking for a match. Little did we know that he had emptied petrol over the rubbish. The next thing we heard was a flash bang, then in he came with flesh rolling down his cheeks.

At that particular time a record was playing on the radio called *Come on Baby Light My Fire* by the Doors' Jim Morrison.

Desperate ride to a darts match

My father made it always clear that he didn't like motorbikes and would never get on one. Anyway one summer evening he was waiting for the bus to get to an important darts match, and for some reason the bus didn't turn up. I pulled up along the kerb to find out what time his bus was when he suddenly said "Come on, give me a lift".

As we went along the road, his gabardine mac was

like a parachute. We came to an S bend and he leaned the wrong way. Eventually we got there, but he was shaking too much from fear to play the match. He had a double brandy and swore he would never again ride on a bike.

Some of the main news events:

Miners strike against Government, strike turns off the lights

Nixon makes historic visit to China

Bloody Sunday report excuses Army

Israeli commanders storm hijacked jet

Protestant march ends in battle

Amin gives Asians 90 days to leave Uganda

Olympic athletes taken hostage and killed in gun battle

National dole strikes begins

Survivors found 10 weeks after plane crash

Earthquake wreaks havoc in Nicaragua

The record that seems to suit the period was *Take Me Back Home*. Other songs that were popular at this time were *Without you, Puppy Love, School's Out, Mama We're All Crazy Now, How Can I Be Sure, Mouldy Old Dough* and *Long Haired Lover from Liverpool.*

1973

In 1973 living in town at my girlfriend's house was great. I was well looked after, and for once I started to feel relaxed. My future mother-in-law could see that I wasn't afraid of work and that I wanted to study.

During this last year of my apprenticeship I surprised some of my fellow colleagues and passed with credit in my last exams. This was all due to the encouragement I got, also room for me to do my homework. I even put some weight on. They treated me like their son, and I was taught how to prepare meals for us after work ready for when they came home.

Very often we would walk up town in the week to go to some of the pubs. I was still working on the shop floor doing the equivalent to some of those on top wages. In the latter part of the year I used to work evenings welding up RSJs for a local businessman - anything to earn extra cash. I even started to help out in the local betting office.

There were various crazy stunts, in one of which I mounted the pavement in town with the girls on the back - I suppose it was showing off, but this was crazy.

Now I can see

Going through the village on my 500cc Triumph I felt on top of the world, as you sometimes do at that stage of your life. One day I picked up a local lad who was very full of himself. I told him always to hold on to the crash bars at the rear. I speeded up and when we got near to the pub I stood up on the bike to get a better view. When we eventually stopped he was frozen with fear.

I was now pretty confident on this bike, which resulted in the most frightening moment in my life. My girlfriend and I went to a town eight miles away on a cold September night, no crash helmets, just the basic gear. I preferred to go back by the country lanes as I had drunk a few. On the main road heading towards the roundabout the throttle was jamming and we went into the bend quicker than usual, leaning over more. The next thing I knew the crash bars had stuck into the road and the bike hurled us across the roundabout.

I was on my back and she was lying face down. I got up and my belt fell off in two pieces. My knee was bleeding and there was grit in my head, but I was almost sick with fright as I thought she had been killed. To my amazement she had only a couple of scrapes and bruises.

We ended up in hospital, and I could hardly speak as my teeth chattered with the shock and cold.

Some of the events of that year:

Britain joins EEC

Nixon orders ceasefire in Vietnam and announces peace deal

Stock Exchange admits women

Nixon takes rap for Watergate scandal

Bomb blasts rock central London

Concorde slashes Atlantic flight time

Dalai Lama makes first UK visit

Arab states attack Israeli forces

Crowds cheer at marriage of Princess Anne

Final deal for thalidomide victims

Picasso the artist dies.

Popular songs included *Come On Feel the Noise, See My Baby, Can the Can, Rubber Bullet, Young Love* and *Welcome Home*.

1974

Now working in the office of the factory and being taught sales work, I had previously done a little in the drawing room. Little did I realise how important this would be to me. I learned about how to cost jobs, labour rates and credit ratings etc. People in the sales office met customers and sometimes took them to lunch - what a change for me. My college days were finished and I wanted to try something on my own and go self employed. I even tried making flower holders which had lead mouldings with pins in, these you would then put in vases and stick the stalks on.

The person I did welding for some evenings was an inspiration for me. One of the new staff who came into the sales team was eventually to play a major part of my life.

Trip home for harvest fair

That summer my girlfriend and I went to a local fair and disco six miles away. We drank plenty and in the background we could hear George McRae singing *Rock me Baby* in the background . We decided we had better get going, and sat astride the bike gripping the 18" high handlebars, my girlfriend hanging on to the crash bars. We pulled out of the car park looking the business, and tore off down the village lanes. I was trying to control the bike and holding on to her as she was sliding about on the seat, and we were heading for this big bend in the road. I could see we were not going to make it.

With one hand on the handlebars and one hand holding her we crashed into the wall, luckily saved by the handlebars and crash bars on the side of the bike. When we eventually stopped she said in a slurred voice, "What have we stopped for – petrol?" My exact words were "We just hit a wall, you stupid bitch!" I still laugh every time I pass that spot.

Later that year I finally sold my Triumph for £30 – it would now be worth over £2,000 - and bought a 650cc BSA Road Rocket which was a different style to others. This had a fibreglass tank, clip-on racing handlebars and goldies (loud exhaust pipes). The bike was red and black and of racing style.

Head-on crash

I normally didn't wear a crash helmet if I could help it, but this day I did. I had some timing problems with the bike, so during dinner time at work I decided to fix it. After putting this right, I decided to give the bike a wind up on the industrial estate main road.

As I was coming down at about 50-60 mph a car in the distance pulled across from a junction into my path. I hit this car head on, shot over the bike and heard a peculiar sound of fluttering birds. I crashed head first into the road, and woke to feel numbness between my legs.

I started crawling under the wreckage, and the young woman in the car, looking totally bewildered, asked what I was doing. I replied "I'm looking for my balls." I knew I had caught them on the large speedometer when I had shot over the bike.

The crash happened outside the factory where I worked, so I left the scene and disappeared into the toilets to drop my pants and see what damage had been done. There was a knock on the door and one of my mates said he would take me to hospital. When I got there I lay back embarrassed when not one but two nurses started using a pencil as lifting gear to inspect me!

When I went home to my lodgings the police arrived to question me. I had to sit on some cushions to ease my problem. The next day I had to see the doctor to register the accident in case I had a future problem in fathering a child.

To top it all, in the afternoon I was walking down the street bow-legged when a young kid shouted out "Hello Marshall Dillon!"

Years later I met the chap who had driven me to hospital that day. He reminded me that he had lost some wages for having time off to take me to hospital. I decided that was the end of bikes for me.

Some of the events of that year were:

Heath calls snap election over miners

Miners' strike comes to an end

Bombs devastate Dublin and Monaghan

Bomb blast at Tower of London and Parliament, four dead in Guildford bomb blast

First female president for Argentina

Bill Shankly quits Liverpool FC

President Nixon resigns

Police hunt Lord Lucan after murder of nanny

Fugitive MP John Stonehouse found alive

Labour scrapes working majority

Records of that time included *Waterloo, Tiger Feet, Seasons in the Sun, Sugar Baby Love, When will I see you again, Kung Fu Fighting, Everything I Own, Lonely this Christmas* and of course *The Streak.*

1975

After the motorbike accident, people were persuading me to learn to drive. I had survived many a crash, but my luck was sure to run out. So I purchased an old Riley 1.5 off a colleague's wife for £60 and started driving lessons.

Work was becoming quite a big responsibility for what we were paid, but we could always do overtime Saturday mornings. We soon found the job was easy and we knew we were approximately half the sales force. My colleague Edward (I said previously that he would play a major role in my life) was sales orientated. We were chalk and cheese from our early days and hadn't liked each other, but now we started to click. We would use our initiative, and if a local job emerged we would slip it through the system and pay off one or two helpers, so Saturday mornings were handy for progressing the homework jobs. We knew the risk but always resented the fact we didn't get more bonus like other staff when we were obtaining orders from our costing and negotiations. We lost a bit of respect for the job.

One day we stayed in town playing pool when the manager came looking for us. When I think of it we were still quite immature in our ways.

What a let-down

Boredom led to the following prank. Day after day in the sales office we were doing the same mundane job and sometimes we needed a laugh. It was a little better if we had visitors or customers. It came to our notice that the chairs that we sat on were adjustable in height - there was a long slot and a large screw to tighten up. If you adjusted it so that the screw was in the edge of the slot it was only a matter of time before the seat would collapse.

One day the Senior Estimator had the Managing Director and Works Manager sitting either side of him in there. He looked across at me and realised that both chairs had been doctored. Just then the Works Manager hit the deck, and the startled director was the next to go a few minutes later. It was sort of cutting them down to size.

We would even play skittles during lunch break. We would use the long corridor, stick up some metal tubes each end and away we would go. Sometimes we would play cards in the toilets in work time.

Some of the events of the year were:

Heiress Lesley Whittle kidnapped

Miners get 35% pay rise

Dozens killed in Moorgate Tube disaster

Charlie Chaplin knighted

Baader Meinhof terrorists blow up embassy

UK embraces Europe in referendum

Arthur Ashe's Wimbledon makes history

Muhammed Ali and the "Thriller in Manila"

Liz Taylor and Richard Burton remarry

Spanish dictator Franco dies

North Sea oil begins to flow

Graham Hill killed flying his own plane

Attack on British vessels heightens Coal War

London Hilton bombed.

Popular songs at this time included *Sailing, Make Me Smile, Oh Boy, Stand By Your Man, I'm Not In Love, Space Oddity, Bohemian Rhapsody, Hold Me Close, DIVORCE, Barbara* and *You Won't Find Another Fool Like Me.*

1976

During this year I passed my driving test, which gave me a bit of independence. But something was about to happen that gave me inspiration. The car failed its MoT on rust, and I was told it was ready for the scrapyard. For 11 hours I stayed under that car, welding it up. When I took it back to the garage he was quite amazed and proceeded to make out my MOT certificate.

I now found myself welding up other people's cars, usually in my brother-in-law's yard or my garage. I could sometimes earn more at the weekends than in the week at work. I mentioned this to Edward at work, who was then my closest associate in the Sales Office, saying I wanted to start up on my own. To this he remarked, why not go into a 50-50 partnership?

Every day we would look through the tenders page, and each of us saved £5 per week towards our great escape. Just before our decision to pair up I went to Middlesex for a welding test with my brother-in-law in my old car. I didn't stay because it meant, unknown to us, that we would have to stay overnight. On the way back I found myself heading into London. I knew I was fresh from passing my test, so I have to admit I did a U-turn. Luckily I avoided trouble.

In the hot summer of 1976 we were continuing to look at tools, but of course you need a workshop. A lady in the sales office at work suggested seeing a middle-aged farmer called Joe a couple of miles away, who lived there as a bachelor with a couple renting a room. One afternoon we met this farmer in the fields and he eventually said we could use his old duck barn by the farm entrance, which would be convenient for deliveries in the future, so we imagined.

Everything was fairly clandestine. We started using and modifying the barn on a Wednesday night and after work we would go for a drink. The farmer didn't take rent off us until we made the decision to do the work full time. We knew it would be a big move, and people hinted that most people who left ended up coming back. It would be a hard thing to move from a nice warm office and a guaranteed weekly pay packet.

Some of the events of 1976:

Iceland and Britain clash at sea over fisheries

Ten dead in Northern Ireland ambush

John Curry takes Olympic skating gold

Harold Wilson resigns as Prime Minister, Callaghan replaces him

Huge earthquake rocks Italy

Israelis rescue Entebbe hostages

Viking spacecraft takes pictures of Mars

Southend Pier engulfed in fire

White rule in Rhodesia to end

Water crisis as taps run dry

Riots at Hull Prison

Notting Hill Carnival ends in riots

Queen opens National Theatre

The music at the time of this blazing hot summer included *I Love to Love, Under the Moon of Love, No Change* (do you mean No Charge?) , *Dancing Queen, Mississippi, Don't Go Breaking my Heart* and finally *Don't Give Up On Us Baby.*

1977

With all the evenings and weekend work I did, I managed to put some money towards getting a bungalow for when my girlfriend and I were getting married. I was not used to cheque books and paid the bills the old-fashioned way. I was careful because I had never had anything on a plate.

As a couple we developed an avid interest in greyhound racing and later on we were to participate.

This was the year we took the car over on the ferry to Ireland. We travelled all round the outskirts and stayed eventually at a cousin's place.

At the racing stand at Shelsbourne Park (Dublin) in the mad rush by some punters I was knocked over and a priest with a fistful of cash walked across my hands while I was on the floor. Then after a late night in a local I was walking back along the dark country roads at 2.30 am when a bus pulled up and offered me a life. He said there would be no charge and gave me a bottle of beer; we opened the top with an opener fixed to the shelf of the bus! I was later told by my auntie that he liked to take the bus home after his night shift.

Meanwhile back at the barn we had to dig a trench

across the farmer's lawn to put a three-phase electric supply into the barn. Luckily there was a pole fairly close, but it still cost us over £700 of our hard-earned savings. The barn itself had old roman tiles on it. The building was approximately 33' x 10'. We put up some sliding doors and knocked a dividing wall out and whitewashed it, but none of this would stop following the wasps coming in from the cider shed next door, the rats coming up the drain and snow getting through the tiles if windy. Even so we loved it.

Later on I was saddened to lose my father-in-law, who had given me such a lot of encouragement.

Some of the events of that year were:

Rock 'n' roll King Elvis Presley dies

Queen celebrates Silver Jubilee

Silent film legend Charlie Chaplin dies

Princess Anne gives birth to a son

Star Wars fever hits Britain

Hat trick for Red Rum

Manchester United sack manager

Hundreds dead in Tenerife plane crash

Firefighters strike over pay claim

Roy Jenkins quits Commons for Brussels

Government wins no confidence vote.

The music was now more disco orientated and included *When I Need You, Knowing Me, Knowing You, Lucille, You Win Again, Yes Sir I Can Boogie, Mull of Kintyre* and *Chanson D'Amour.*

1978

For the next three or four years my wife and I got involved in greyhound racing, and we went as often as our pockets would let us. I eventually built a large galvanised sheet shed at bottom of the garden - the neighbours were not impressed. This shed was sufficient to house at least three dogs. We even bought a pup and were having it trained, but eventually it had to be put down due to illness.

High-speed cabinet

While I was still working in the sales office a humorous incident occurred. I was working in an open plan office with three colleagues and a sales manager who had his own office. I already had a couple of dogs and saw in a magazine that there was one I liked for sale, in Shelbourne Park, Dublin. BT had been in to sort a fault out but had made a blunder, leaving my phone on an outside line, so I could bypass the switchboard.

Well one morning I hung my drawings up around me so I was enclosed to study them for quoting purposes. I was talking to the owner of this dog in Ireland when he explained that it was black with four white legs, I suddenly realised the Manager was looking over me. He asked if I meant what I had I said. I said it was a black cabinet on four white pillars. His comment was that this sounded a bit Irish to me, and he left looking perplexed. I never did get the dog as it was beyond my reach financially, but at least I had the outside line to try again.

There were numerous occasions when I got the bookies (for whom I did part-time work) to put the phone over the speaker so I could hear the race commentary on my phone. In our private lives the greyhound racing kept us together, as we both loved it.

I joined a great skittle team which proved almost unbeatable. We usually played Thursday nights, and as young men do sometimes we drank too much and ended up at the local night club. These nights we could afford because of the extra money we earned at the would-be future workshop.

The town was now still pretty lively, but the motorbike scene was never the same as it was, and of course we were older.

Some of the events of that year were:

Saddam in US for Middle East talks

Egyptian forces die in Cyprus gunfight

Tories recruit advertisers to win votes

Carter wins Panama Canal battle and
delays N-bomb production

Naomi James takes world sailing record

Four dead in Post Office shootings
Botham bowls his way into cricket history
First test tube baby born
Sex Pistols' Sid Vicious on murder charge
Mass suicide leaves 900 dead
Spain set for democracy.

Some of the songs playing that year were *Wuthering Heights, Night Fever, Three Times a Lady, Summer Nights, Rat Trap, Rivers of Babylon* and *Figaro.*

KJ as a boy

Rebellious youth

At last I had got what I wanted

The start of my motorbiking days

My childhood in the 1960s

The mansion on the moors where a duck shed
was converted into our factory

At work

With my son

The factory

Feeling fit at 50

I GOTTA HORSE

Steve Dennis meets Jim Kilduff who is overcoming life's heartaches with Wild Ground

Champions at last as the dream unfolds

Horse Wild Ground **Career wins** 6
Owners Jim Kilduff & Ken Jones
Best day When the dream came true at Fontwell

ONCE upon a time there was a horse called Aldaniti and a man named Bob Champion. You know all about them. Now there's a horse named Wild Ground and a man called Jim Kilduff, and although we aren't dealing in Grand Nationals the stories aren't so very far apart.

Wild Ground is a 12-year-old mare with a history of misfortune. "She's had a sinus operation, she struck into herself, then she had heat in one of her good legs, and to top it all she picked up a hairline fracture in her pelvis," says Kilduff.

Kilduff, 60, has Parkinson's disease, but he doesn't let it affect him, and it had been his dream to own a racehorse since the age of eight when visits to the local clinic due to his asthma led to his initiation into the sport.

"My Dad used to take me to the clinic and on the way back we'd stop at the pub," he says. "I remember all the talk about horses – when I looked at their names in the paper it helped me relax, eased my asthma."

Kilduff liked a bet, liked sitting

Wild Ground has been a revelation for her connections this season

with his grandfather in the shed and listening to the results on the radio in the evening. He had a penchant for tricasts, remembers well getting the 1-2-3 in the 1981 Grand National when Aldaniti led them home. And he still had the dream of owning a horse.

"The chance came with Wild Ground," he says. "I went to Kevin Bishop because he was local and they're nice people, straightforward.

"I bought the mare and had money for training fees, went halves with my son Dan. He dropped out after a while and my friend Ken Jones took his share."

Later, though, frustrated by Wild Ground's problems, Kilduff thought about cutting his losses. "All I'd done was pay out," he says. "But Kevin told me he'd get her right and would train her for free until she won a race."

Wild Ground returned from almost two years off, was pulled up at Taunton and then went to Fontwell

last month for a long-distance chase. She won by 45 lengths.

"I didn't go," chuckles Kilduff. "I wasn't feeling great that day so I watched in the bookies, and when she crossed the line my jaw hit the floor.

"It had been a miserable couple of years, what with my condition and the fact that my brother Tony and my brother-in-law Barry had both died.

"It was Barry who told me not to give up, that the mare would win a race one day. That day in the bookies it was like he was staring down through the clouds at me."

Wild Ground – who while she was on the easy list foaled a colt by Helissio, now three years old and waiting for Kilduff to give him a good name – won again at Fontwell later that month. It'll all be in Kilduff's book one day; it'll be some read.

"It's been my dream come true," he says. "Sometimes they do, don't they?"

1979

This was the year we prepared everything mentally and physically to turn the barn into a workshop. We formed a three-way partnership, without which we might never have had the final push that was needed to get us started. We were trained sheet metal workers taking on fabrication, which would be like a new trade. Luckily we knew how to cost jobs and read drawings.

Going back to my studying geometry in the shed, little did I know that this was to save us thousands in drawing fees, while my partner and colleague had the techniques of a salesman.

The idea of the three-way partnership was that the third partner, Toby, who was already in business, would supply steel drawing and we would do it for a reasonable rate, but this was the plan for when we were to start. Of course we had to open up accounts, see the bank etc.

Whenever a supplier turned up at the factory we would collar them. Second hand machinery sales helped us out with the basics such as saws, welding etc. It was a big decision because we were as I have said in comfortable jobs with security. The real world was just round the corner.

There was to be a rude awakening, as we were to be forced to group up. and to make matters worse there was a steel strike looming. Even so we were excited.

That year nothing odd happened other than getting my fingers trapped in the car door. A friend of mine had just dropped me off, and he took off with me running alongside trying to get his attention. Obviously I succeeded or it could have messed up all my plans.

Some of the headlines that year:

Margaret Thatcher elected first woman Prime Minister

Shah of Iran flees into exile

Exiled Ayatollah Khomeini returns for victory as army steps aside

China invades Vietnam

Car bomb kills Airey Neave

Jeremy Thorpe cleared of murder charges

Kurdish revolt grows in Iran

IRA bomb kills Lord Mountbatten

Soldiers die in Warren Point massacre

Anthony Blunt revealed as 'fourth man'

Council tenants get right to buy

The Times returns after year-long absence.

Music of the time included *Heart of Glass, I Will Survive, I Don't Like Mondays, Message in a Bottle, Walking on the Moon* and *When You're in Love With a Beautiful Woman.*

1980

At the beginning of 1980 you could say that I and my business partner were like turkeys in November. We finally announced the date we intended to work as a three-way partnership, which was March 6th. It was all agreed prior to leaving. The third parties would supply a certain amount of steel per month for us to cover our business financially.

On the day we started, the driveway outside the workshop was covered in 20' – 30' girders and the farmer had to use the field to get through. The weather was atrocious and eventually we hired a crane to shift the steel into a sensible place. Straight away we were £60 down.

Suddenly we realised that this was the real world. We looked at each other and asked "What have we done?", but we did not want to give up to easily as we both had commitments to mortgages etc, plus there was a bit of pride at stake.

Everything from unloading to loading was done by hand and the work was very physical because we had to produce so much in a limited time. It was a total shock to the body after our sedate jobs. We knew we had to go on as a two-way partnership as the third parties were not always using us to manufacture, but we knew this lot. After all everything was on trust.

Some of the steelwork wasn't coming to us as planned, so we eventually had a meeting and the two of us paid him off and went into partnership in our own names. By now we were over £6,000 overdrawn, desperate for work and with winter on our doorstep.

We did a lot of assorted metalware for the holiday camps. I designed a casing for a number of shower box meters, which stopped people breaking in to extract the cash. Word of mouth and the odd advert kept us going. Given all the worry, we were content, but we obviously needed a good customer. We knew we had to sell ourselves in character, knowledge and integrity to someone who might take a chance giving work to young blokes working in a barn on the moors. We just needed that lucky break.

In the meantime we would travel about to the odd customer and measure up projects, and I would take home the details and work out the requirements for the steel that was needed and the cutting list ready for the next day.

On a lighter note, occasionally at about 3 pm the farmer would call us into the brewing shed and we would drink a pint of almost green cider. We had to socialise as he was a bachelor farmer helping us out, not many of his kind.

When things were quiet we set up cricket stumps

with our painter and labourer and played cricket. It was paradise in the summer, so peaceful and serene we hardly saw a car or a person some days. Most days it was just us and occasionally the painter. We had to trust him and rely on each other. The last thing we needed was any of us being ill.

Music at the time included *Starting Over, Crying, Atomic, The Tide is High, The Winner Takes It All, Don't Stand So Close To Me* and *Use it Up and Wear it Out.*

Some headlines from 1980:

Mugabe to lead independent Zimbabwe

North Sea oil platform collapses

SAS rescue ends Iranian embassy siege

War breaks out between Iran and Iraq

Pope welcomes Queen to Vatican

John Lennon shot dead

1981

I was getting very involved with work as after all we wanted to survive. My marriage was now showing cracks through faults on both sides. We had silly disputes over the running of the dogs and me bringing drawings home to work on, even household bills, but nothing seemed to be serious. We were always out in the evenings, going somewhere or socialising.

By now we were developing a unique partnership. My partner could be great at the salesmanship and giving the customer confidence in us, while I would answer some of the technical questions when measuring up, such as where a staircase would pitch etc.

In those early days my colleague never stopped looking for work and I was happy to draw it up. There had to be harmony to survive. I would tend to lean towards my colleague's decisions because he was the salesman in the partnership and was obviously in liaison with the customers more, but I would assume designs and draw up and order the steel while my partner handled the invoices and cheques. These were two paths that gradually developed but everything was as agreed 50-50.

Before we purchased a works van we had an old Morris Minor we used to scoot around in, looking for different work locations. I was to ask for directions if we were stuck but I was always reminded by my partner not to laugh, though we always ended up in fits. Other things I recall include siphoning fuel off if we were low.

A day at the betting office
I helped out on a Saturday in a local betting office. I used to mark the prices up on the sheets for each race and when the result came in, write with a felt pen the names of the horses and the betting odds. One day I was writing the names up and wrote the first name backwards because the woman who worked there had distracted me by leaning over the table and exposing her skimpy underwear. Several of the customers were wondering what was happening, but any hot-blooded male who had seen what I had seen would be distracted.

The greyhound shed
I was now living in a bungalow on the outskirts of town and used to work hard and play hard. One evening my wife and I went out and I drank plenty of beer in town. I went out at closing time to drive the car into a side street and ploughed the car into the landlord's car and his son's brand new car. My bonnet flew up and the lights fell out.

The landlord was frantic and suggested I came back and sorted out the problem tomorrow. To avoid the police I drove back via the back roads on a one way system the opposite way with no lights on and my head out of the window to see my way home. It was crazy.

The next day, after my wife had gone to work, I got up to see the police pulled up outside. I jumped out of the bedroom window and ran down to the shed where the two greyhounds were. All I had on was my pants. I sat in with the dogs with both hands over their mouths trying to keep them quiet, but their tails were hitting the galvanised sheeting of the shed.

The policeman came towards the shed and called out if I was in there. I said I had had to feed the dogs, to which he said when he had seen me in my pants and they must be desperate. I was expecting the worst, but he then asked if I could go round to his place and measure some steelwork for him!

Dogs on the run

I was at work one day when a neighbour rang in and explained that my two greyhounds were on the loose in a field where sheep were grazing. I tore home and went searching for them. When I got over the gate the field was dotted with tufts of fleece everywhere. The field looked like the view from an aeroplane window. Obviously the dogs had been chasing the sheep them around. The sheep were lying down bleating and exhausted. I managed to get the dogs in. If the farmer had been around he would have shot them.

A lucky break finally came when we did part-time

sales work for certain factories that had gone bust. To compensate us the managers of this firm put a customer on to us who visited us with drawings to quote to. He finally decided before he went that a game of cricket in the yard would be nice. He took away a few notes about us and left drawings for us to price, which we did very carefully. A few days later he gave us the first of many orders, for Sothebys. We were now on cloud nine and this was make or break.

Some of the events of that year were:

Prince Charles and Lady Diana to marry

President Reagan shot and injured

Bobby Sands dies in prison

Thousands see Pope shot in Rome

Bangladeshi president assassinated

Mystery disease kills homosexuals

Steel workers strike over pay

Teheran frees US hostages after 444 days

Gun battle at British Embassy in Iraq

Reagan beats Carter in landslide election

Michael Foot is new Labour Leader

The songs of the time included *Ghost Train, Tainted Love, Japanese Boy, Jealous Guy, Woman,* and finally two records which seemed to relate to our new customer, *Make Your Mind Up and Stand and Deliver.*

1982

At last we had a good customer, as well as a few smaller customers. This customer's steelwork was mainly 20' lay girders, 150 kg each with supporting steel post staircases etc. In a typical order we would throw the girders off the lorry on to tractor tyres and stack them up in rows. Eventually we would lift them up physically on to a trolley, tie it outside the workshops and work on them come rain or shine, as there wasn't much room inside. Finally we had a friend who came in and swiftly got the red or grey paint on. I finally made two frames that would rest against the side of the lorry. To load the job we would lift each girder up to these frames, get behind the steel and push it up to where my colleague and the driver would stack the steel neatly on the lorry. Doing this sort of work with no fork lift was risky as this was heavy work, but we were keen. We didn't even insure ourselves.

These were the toughest times of our lives but the most happy and rewarding. We were strong and I even had my first proper sun tan. But conditions in the winter were atrocious because we were so exposed on the moors. Regularly in the morning we had to pour hot water on the bottom door rollers. We even kept a bottle of brandy in the workshop, because the steel was either frosted or covered in snow.

In the summer we loved it. It was serene and tranquil, not like the mundane industrial estate, and hardly anyone knew where we were. The owner left us alone except when his dog went astray and drove the sheep into the ravines, when our help was required. Other than that, if the pressure was not on we would play of stint of cricket, then sometimes go and join the farmer for a cider. The highlight of the day would always be when Norman's car came into the drive with another job.

I hope I have given an insight into the surroundings we were working in. We never even had planning permission, because we were so isolated hardly anyone knew of us.

I acquired a nicer car, but got caught in it for drink driving - at least four or five police cars finally caught up with me at home. My son Daniel was born this year, but my father became worse.

Funny things would often happen on site. A pair of moleskins came down over my head because I was engrossed in ogling a sensational beauty on the lawn, and another time a scantily-clad French woman was parading around the flat where I was measuring windows for ornamental ironwork.

Some of the events that year were:

Laker Airways goes bust

Argentina invades Falklands, Britain regains control

Queen fends off bedroom intruder

IRA bombs cause carnage in London

Mary Rose rises after 437 years at the
bottom of the sea

Mother jailed in dingo baby murder

Solidarity leader Lech Walesa released

Armed activists bomb Downing Street.

The music we were listening to included *Do You Really Want to Hurt Me, House of Fun, Land of Make Believe, The Eye of the Tiger* and *Come on Eileen.*

1983

We had a policy, which both of us tried to adhere to, that we would not tell the worker what to do and ask nothing of him that we had not done ourselves. I always felt later that anyone going to work for us should be content. I know this cannot always happen on a larger scale.

In my private life I was still not settled. I always felt that the lowly-paid apprenticeship days had robbed me of some fun. The town pub I used to use in early seventies had now become, as they say, buzzing again, and pool games were very popular, with a league on a Sunday night, and of course there was always the night club, which seduced me and was really the cause of me being banned from driving.

I felt I had worked hard and had a little cash and was going to enjoy myself at times. It was work hard, play hard. But of course now I was banned from driving, I started to use taxis regularly.

The odd customer would come in for cider sampling the goods, and we would watch them reverse up the drive into of the posts even, though there was enough room for a 40 ton articulated lorry to fit.

The farmer used to fuss and spoil his dog, though

sometimes he would be chasing the dog with a stick, shouting out "I'll kill thee!" usually when his trusted pet drove some more sheep into the ravine.

Our painter lad and I were down on our main customer unit, turning over large sheets of heavy plate approx 8' x 4' when I acquired a false hand from a shop clear out. One day as the plate slammed down I casually slipped the hand on to the floor and withdrew my arm with my hand up my sleeve. He turned white with shock, but he had the last laugh because weeks later while he sat in the car I was shutting our doors and some metal parts came down and cut my leg. He thought I was playing around again and just looked at me.

The Sting

There was now a chance of a big job for the Middle East. We knew we needed some code welding certificates, which we achieved, but the client suggested we rigged up his factory unit and made it as though we produced the job there. Obviously we would produce it at our premises and transport it to the unit for final inspection. One time we didn't have transport and the only way was for the farmer to deliver by tractor and trailer.

Finally the customer's inspectors came to view. We had to quickly clean up some of the cow dung that was splattered here and there, obviously incurred down the country lanes, and this nearly blew our chances on other stages of the job. But we did finish the job and money wasn't so tight afterwards, at least for a while.

Some of the events that year were:

BBC wakes up to morning TV

British drivers ordered to belt up

Police hunt Shergar kidnappers

Bristol police on trail of mass murderer

Hitler 'diaries' published

Thatcher wins landslide victory

Dozens escape in Maze Prison break out

Dennis Nielsen murders

US troops invade Grenada

£25m gold heist at Heathrow

Transplant makes British medical history

TV cameras allowed into House of Lords

CND March attracts biggest ever crowd.

The music which was playing included *Wherever I Lay My Hat, Give It Up, Let's Dance, Pipes of Peace, Every Breath I Take, Uptown Girl, Red Red Wine, True, Down Under, Too Shy, Karma Chameleon.*

1984

This year is a year I would rather forget if I could. We had by now another mainstream customer which entailed us getting a lot more tooling up. We now had to look after the main customers where our regular work came from, which really kept the bills paid, and gone were the days when we could do the odd jobs, or if we could they usually had to wait. When work was quiet we would often go for a drive, calling somewhere for lunch or breakfast. Back at the workshop we would play silly games such as turning a woolly hat over a gas bottle or even a little cricket.

Then came a tragedy. One cold Cheltenham Gold Cup Day the farmer was out across the fields and we were taking a break when all of a sudden we heard cries of help from the farmhand, who was exhausted from running. He said the farmer had hitched the tractor up too high and it had turned over on him.

We drove down to the sport and four or five of us managed to lift the tractor off him, but we could find nothing to wedge under it. It was a terrible sight. The sirens eventually arrived, but of course he had been killed outright. We went back to the workshop and had a shot of brandy each, realising that our days on the moors were numbered.

The farmer's brother came out, and he had a totally different nature. He gave us a few months to find another place. Then one morning we were sitting on the edge of the workshop floor when a car pulled up and two blokes dressed rather smartly got out. They were planning officers, who had come to tell us we had to apply for planning permission.

Later that year my marriage was over. I was quite devastated and very depressed. My colleagues tried to boost my morale, as my self esteem was low, and work was still important - I didn't want to lose everything. I even went to a health farm for a week as a treat.

After one drinking session I took a short cut across a paddock in the rain and in the morning my brother-in-law walked in the front door and found a trail of mud and brambles to my bedroom. I had obviously had trouble with a hedge.

Some of the events of that year were:

Miners strike over threatened job closures

Dozens arrested in picket line violence

Arthur Scargill vetoes national ballot on strikes

Libyan Embassy shot kills policewoman
Yvonne Fletcher

President Reagan arrives in China

Scientist identify Aids virus

Moscow pulls out of US Olympics
Tory Cabinet in Brighton bomb blast
US Embassy blast kills 20
UK and China agree to Hong Kong handover
Violence follows Gandhi killing
London tube fire traps hundreds
Gorbachev visits Britain
Court fines Scargill for obstruction.

Music at the time included *99 Red Balloons, Relax, Careless Whisper, Power of Love, Freedom, Two Tribes, I Just Called To Say I Love You, Wake Me Up Before You Go Go, Hello* and *Pipes of Peace.*

1985

Depression - I suppose everyone tastes a slice of this. Over the next three or four years I suffered low self-esteem followed by depression, which when on your own living can lead to over indulgence of alcohol, but I wasn't working for someone else - I had to remind myself that I still had responsibilities to partnerships and the lads who now worked for us.

We relocated to a unit on the industrial estate which dwarfed the shed we had been in. We were now in a more professional environment, which involved building a new office and advertising. The rent jumped from £11 per week to over £100 per week, but we were now capable of producing large steel-framed buildings with the extra space we acquired. We also had a fork lift truck, and all these extra overheads were met through new customers.

During this year we came across an ex-steel erector we called TM from up north, who consumed a fair amount of scotch, but came in and did some labouring. He was old school, assorted lunch box, brylcreemed hair, yes sir, no sir. He would come in sometimes the worse for wear due to the previous night's drinking, but he would sing to the tapes of the fifties and was good at making the tea. On one occasion, after several pleas for him to make the tea, he did so only to walk in to the workshop and suddenly go sprawling across the floor. He had managed to trip over the fork lift. When we remarked that after all that he had spilt the tea, he was spitting bricks. He was similar to Stan Laurel in appearance, and we would play a record by Johnny Mathis called *A Certain Smile*, which would have a calming influence on him.

Later that year I was under pressure to sell up and sort out my financial obligations. Luckily I had support from my partner on this matter, and assistance in acquiring a flat in a nearby town.

In the meantime my son Daniel was now three years old. I used to pick him up at weekends and sometimes I brought him into work on Saturday mornings. He would come to me until I finished paying maintenance when he was 18 years old.

In November we survived a head-on crash after a car careered over a bridge on the wrong side of the road. I could not steer clear because there was a pond below, so I let go of the steering wheel and heaved myself swiftly between my son and the windscreen, as he was standing up between the seats. Luckily on this occasion I didn't have my seat belt on. That incident still haunts me.

The headlines of 1985 included:

Miners call off year-long strike

Gorbachev becomes Soviet Leader

Four killed in Bradford Stadium fire

UEFA bans English clubs from Europe

Boris Becker wins Wimbledon at 17

Live Aid makes millions for Africa

Heart and lung transplant makes history

Titanic wreck found and filmed after 73 years

Riots in Brixton after police shooting

Policeman killed in Tottenham riots

Commandos storm hijacked plane

Mexico suffer a devastating earthquake

Volcano kills thousands in Columbia.

Music at the time included *I Want to Know What Love Is, I Know Him So Well, Into The Groove, Move Closer, Power of Love, Easy Lover, A Good Heart, I Am Your Man, Saving All My Love For You* and *Dancing in the Street.*

1986

My partner agreed to help me out back on to the housing ladder as he would probably be looking to move later. Luckily work was OK and I managed to obtain a one bedroom flat on the sea front, on the top floor. The other two flats on this floor were empty. Because I was self employed with good accounts this without doubt saved me renting as my settlement wasn't good financially.

When I moved in, it was very ornate and tasteful as the previous owner had been an antique dealer. The view over the sea front was beautiful, and to the side I could see the church gardens, where the public could go and sit at their leisure, which led me to this silly prank.

Playing the bones

As I was getting used to my flat overlooking the beautiful gardens that summer, I would come home at dinner time, cook chops and potatoes and eat my dinner in the kitchen looking out over the gardens, where many people were sitting around with their dogs. Once I had devoured my dinner the wastage was basically a couple of bones. Giving in to temptation, I opened the window a little more, closed the blinds a little and tossed the bones out of the window. All hell would break loose as dogs fought for them and people ranted.

After having to start life by myself in this flat, I embarked on a policy of work hard and play hard. Any spare cash usually went on taxis. I kept myself to myself, not being in a frame of mind to trust anyone, but played in the local pool team and skittle team.

Depression still bothered me. Drink was not the answer, but it used to help you forget the worst for a while. The only trouble I had with the flat was at night when the wind would howl around, then seagulls in the early morning would walk on the flat roof. Then to top it all off the church bells would chime in, so on most occasions I drank more alcohol. The brandy bottle was beside my bed, and sometimes I would swig a couple of shots first thing in the morning.

Holiday to Spain

Knowing the current state of my mind, a holiday abroad would do me good, and one or two of my friends thought how I had only been to Ireland until now. They say travel broadens the mind – well, the following escapade I wasn't going to reveal but I thought it was a typical example when indulgences in alcohol and strangers mix.

I travelled by myself to Fuengirola, with my partner and his family coming over a week later. As soon as I arrived I could see it was a lively place and a good atmosphere, though after a couple of days the hotel held onto my passport, which incensed me.

I settled in and enjoyed the beach and the beers.

One evening after about three days I decided to wander up the back street bars, drinking brandy. The next day I realised I was waking up in a stranger's home! I was half dressed lying in a four poster bed when a red-haired Spanish woman approached from behind some hanging beads, and started calling me a typical tourist. Then she said she would get her ex-husband from the secret police to deal with me. I looked around and found every access locked up. I said I had friends coming over, as I knew I had just a couple of hours to get away, but she didn't believe I was staying at a hotel. Eventually I convinced her after seeing a six figure phone number on the new paper similar to the hotel I was staying at, and by now she was more amicable and decided to let me out.

I found myself on a hillside, miles from anywhere. I was hot and also skint, and generally lost. I strolled down this rough track when I began to hear music. Around the bend I saw a shack. I entered the shack and an American wearing a large white sombrero arranged for a taxi to get me back to my hotel, which was about 6.5 kilometres away.

Back at the hotel they gave me back my passport and showed me a picture of a terrorist who resembled me. Apparently I was being watched over a couple of days. The whole episode just seemed so surreal.

Back home work was going quite well, and we were on the verge of a very important new customer and employing useful staff.

Some of the events that year were:

US launches air strikes in Libya

Bomb tears a hole in airliner over Greece
after another bomb kills 21 in Sri Lanka

Ian Paisley battle cry condemned,
Orange parade sparks riots

Prince Andrew marries Sarah Ferguson

Karachi hijack ends in bloodshed

UK cuts links with Syria over bomb plot

Evil Jeremy Bamber jailed for murders

Harold Macmillan dies

Oil workmen die in helicopter crash.

The music at this time included *The Sun Always Shines On TV, Don't Leave Me This Way, Final Countdown, Edge of Heaven, Papa Don't Preach, Lady in Red, Take My Breath Away, Caravan of Love* and *Spirit In The Sky.*

1987

Over the next three or four years life was quite traumatic. I was to lose my dad this year and my grandparents and cousin the next year, as well as incurring some hefty debts. I found the flat I lived in comfortable but there was always a sense of isolation, which encouraged me to venture out to the town most nights. Three or four local lads became great mates with me, but because of my emotional problems it took a little to break the ice with me. The trouble with my policy of working hard and playing hard was that it occasionally led me to embarrassing moments.

Wrong door

After a heavy night out and the worse for wear, I was struggling to get up the three flights of steps which I had laid down outside the door temporarily. I arrived at my door on the third level in a stupor. I more or less came to when I tried to unlock the door, to no avail. I was getting so desperate for the toilet I that I decided to ram the door in. At the third attempt the door suddenly opened and I went flat out on the floor, with my neighbour a military man) glaring down at me.

"You are Number 9, not Number 6!" he said. I had misread it. Very embarrassing. You could say I was about as popular as a rattlesnake in a lucky dip. It just goes to show the problems drink can bring on.

Stand by me

We now had four lucrative customers, the latest being a loft conversion firm. There were now at least five of us and sometimes outside help came in. We treasured those customers and virtually never let them down on deliveries - after all time can mean money.

We got a four-wheel drive for me as a work tool and private use – I eventually got through eight of them over the next 20 years. We became a close-knit band of workmen and would treat our workmates to days out.

Beaujolais Day

Every year around the third week in November when the Beaujolais Nouveau arrived we would shut up the workshop for the day and at midday go to the local inn to celebrate Beaujolais Day. This was a day which attracted all walks of life. As the day wore on you could see caution thrown to the winds. By six o'clock some people were hanging over the rail outside being sick, some were half asleep, and flirting was at its peak.

By evening, after several taxis had been organised, I eventually headed back to town and a few more drinks later, a friend offered me a lift home, which was great except that when I was in the car I could not remember where I lived, so I went back to his house for a while. Later when I resurrected my memory I was taken home. I remember sitting at the top of the stairs undoing my laces. The next thing I knew I woke up at the bottom. There were black shoe marks down the wall like something out of a cartoon, but no injuries. The most harmful thing was the slate we ran up at the pub.

Some of the events that year were:

Peace envoy Terry Waite imprisoned in Beirut

Cynthia Payne accused of running brothels

Synod says yes to women priests

Hundreds drown as Herald of
Free Enterprise capsizes

Thatcher wins record third term

Nazi war criminal Klaus Barbie gets life

Gunman kills 14 in Hungerford rampage

Superpower treaty to scrap warheads

Lester Piggott jailed for three years

Newspaper caught in spycatcher row

Van Gogh painting fetches record price

Kings Cross Station crash kills 27.

Hit songs at this time included *Nothing Gonna Stop Us Now, Everything I Own, You Win Again, Never Gonna Give You Up, You Were Always On My Mind, La Bamba, I Wanna Dance With Somebody, I Just Can't Stop Loving You, It's A Sin* and *Respectable*.

1988

This was the year my partner helped me to get back into a bigger house in the town, which definitely felt more sociable. During this year we grew up in business. We realised you have to cross your T's and dot your I's. We took a job on through the winter, only to find after four months that the customer had decided not to pay us on a technicality, due to the steel issued by them. The sum was over £13,000 plus our solicitor's bill of £1,200, and we never got a penny.

The firm started up again under another name and we toiled all summer to try and recuperate. We kept a low profile, in case people got the impression that we might not be safe to deal with. We were getting back on our feet when in the September of this year we took another financial blow of over £8,000. This was bad, because it was mainly steel cost and of course the word 'trust' comes into the equation. To make it worse, these were locals.

All the work and worry led me to developing shingles, which was painful, but I could not really take time off work. On the comical side I had to have a purple lotion applied to my back three times a day. One day in the office I was bent forward with my shirt over my head allowing my partner to apply this lotion when in came one of our customers, looking totally bemused.

Otherwise nothing happened of much importance. My mates and I were members of a local club which occasionally organised a day out at the races.

Events that year included:

Jumbo jet crashes on Lockerbie

Nurses protest for better pay

IRA suspects shot dead in Gibraltar

USSR pledges to leave Afghanistan

'Ivan the Terrible' guilty of war crimes

US warship shoots down Iranian airliner

Piper Alpha oil rig ablaze

Gold for Johnson in 100m sprint

Latvia cries freedom from Moscow

Government loses Spycatcher battle

Egg industry fury over salmonella claim

35 dead in Clapham rail collision.

The hits at the time included *I Owe You Nothing, With a Little Help From My Friends, He Ain't Heavy, He's My Brother, I Think We Are Alone Now, One Moment In Time, Perfect, Heaven is a Place On Earth, The Only Way Is Up* and *Crazy Kind of Love.*

1989

Still reeling from debts, we began to realise how important the two or three good customers we had were, so you could say we would jump to their attention. If another customer came to us it suddenly put us on our guard and we would state conditions that would suit us, with a deposit etc. Instinct would soon tell you if they were OK.

One of the bigger worries was if you got in too deep with one customer and they were maybe a little slow on paying. They could dictate your cash flow and in some cases had too much control if they subbed work to you. But the nineties would see us climbing out of the hard times to make some good money, paying loads of tax for our effort.

I moved home again with the consent of my business partner, who in turn had some conversions done. There was a clash of personalities with my new neighbour, who was very old school, a rather large intimidating woman with an echoing voice.

The lawn ranger
I had just moved into a fairly new house, it was a

Saturday afternoon and the horse racing was on the television. It was a nice sunny day, so I put the television out in the long grass with a few cans of lager to consume at my leisure. I was nice and settled when my neighbour bent over the fence and said I would never get the grass cut like that. At this I got up and started to scatter beer on the grass. She asked me curiously what I was up to, and I said that I was hoping it would come up half cut.

Later when my son was there I decided to cut it. There was an old ditch covered in weeds and brambles behind the fence across the bottom of the garden. When I had finished the last bit, I wanted to push it craftily into the ditch, so I bent over the fence to heave the grass cuttings over when the fence panel broke and I was propelled head first into the ditch.

I crawled out covered in green slime and brambles, and my son said that the last thing he saw was a pair of white trainers. In the heat the panels had shrunk and the fixings were more pliable.

Fatal distraction

One sunny afternoon I got into my four wheel drive parked up in the driveway when a neighbour appeared in just a bikini, stretching up on tiptoe to water the hanging baskets. Naturally I was taking in the view, and I was so engrossed that I reversed out and ploughed into the neighbour's car opposite, causing £400 worth of damage. Luckily all was resolved amicably - just another lesson on keeping you eyes in the right place.

During the summer of this year a lady friend moved in with me. This would be nice for a while, but what did I know of her? Meeting someone in a public house is not always the best way to choose a partner.

Headlines of 1989

Soviet troops pull out of Afghanistan

Exxon Valdez creates oil slick disaster

Football fans crushed at Hillsborough

Princess Diana opens landmark Aids Centre

Marchioness river crash kills 30

Anglican anger over united church

East German leader ousted

Berlin celebrates the fall of the Berlin Wall

New era for Czechoslovakia after Ceausescus shot

Mueller summit ends cold war

Thatcher beats of leadership threat.

The music at this time included *Ride on Time, All Around the World, Eternal Flame, Sealed With a Kiss, Let's Party, Like a Prayer, Something's Gotta Hold of My Heart* and *Too Many Broken Hearts.*

1990

During our time together the new girlfriend and I acquired an eight-week-old Old English Sheepdog, but our relationship was not to last. We did not part without some friction as the lady in question decided to go to a solicitor to see if she could claim something off me, and this unnerved me for the future. But we had some good memories, such as the day I took her to Royal Ascot and she looked stunning. That day I consumed five or six cans of lager and was randomly stopped on the way home. I took the breathalyser test and 40 seconds later was told I was clear. It was irresponsible, but I just got too wrapped up in the day.

We treated the staff to a day out, with GKN reps getting tickets to Wincanton Races. It gave me pleasure to see the lads having a day out.

The nineties were the days when we saved for our pensions, but as we were getting older the work seemed to be of a larger nature and wanted more quickly.

Leisure time meant a Sunday Night Pool League and mixed skittle team. My partner and I used to book up to see a band or artist coming up, to ensure we took some time away from the pressure of work.

A birthday surprise

This particular birthday I went out to our local club for a few beers and game of pool. All of a sudden as I was playing pool a record started playing called Hot in the City Tonight. The next thing I knew I was approached by a scantily-dressed blonde who was very tidy, as we say. The next I knew I was on the floor in a chair with her starkers over me. Of course there was an audience. She enticed me to pluck items from her body with my mouth.

A special darts match came to a halt and everyone was peering through the windows. There were even people coming in off the street, and the windows and wine cabinet were all steamed up. On top of that a lot of the elderly gents were flushed and confused. Later I found the steward had thought the booking was a kissogram and not a strippergram.

The next day I went to buy some ham and the young woman in the shop said "You sure you don't want marshmallows? Of course you eat them differently to most people". The night before I had been eating marshmallows off the stripper's breast, and word had travelled. I still have some of the more decent photographs that were taken that night.

Luckily some of my mates were always there for me. As one of them said, "Stay single and hear your money jingle". By now, thanks to some of what had happened to me, I was drinking plenty, to such an extent that the Medical Centre asked me back to give another sample as the one they had had solidified in transit. This had never happened before, they said.

But work was still my priority. More blokes and bigger jobs meant more paperwork, invoices and deliveries, though I was still active on the shop floor. I still tended to get the steel on order with best prices, delivery dates etc. We knew we couldn't trust anyone who offered to take the pressure off, as we were to learn later on.

Some of that year's headlines

De Klerk dismantles apartheid in South Africa

Freedom for Nelson Mandela

Violence flares in poll tax demonstrations

Flexible telescope takes off for space

Yeltsin resignation splits Soviet Communism

Ireland elects first woman president

Thatcher forced out as Prime Minister,
Major for Number 10

Major proposes new Euro currency

Iraq frees British hostages.

Hit songs that year included *Tears On My Pillow, Little Time, The Joker, Sacrifice, Killer, Nothing Compares To You, Ice Ice Baby, Vogue, The Power* and *Hanging Touch.*

1991

In the early part of this year I was involved in another relationship which came about through the pool league. She was 16 years younger than me, and I realised a little later that the trouble here was her differences with her ex. One evening at the night club I had an altercation with him after a few too many, but it became more serious when the bouncers decided they would propel me down the stairs head first. The upshot of all this was special surgery for a few hours, then 26 weeks of physiotherapy.

When in hospital I was in severe pain and realised that the medical team probably looked on me as not so important as the incoming accident victims. I felt at a low ebb in my life and realised I might not get the use of my arm back. This incident still bothers me because of pain at night when lying on my side, but when you live by the sword you die by it.

Things were a little tight financially after suffering bad debts, and to keep us going we had a small loan, because at the end of the day the tax man doesn't want to know your problems. When I reflect on it we never got any help when starting up. All of a sudden when we got established they wanted a slice.

We heard on the grapevine that there was an industrial unit coming up for sale, which was what we had always yearned for, to do away with rent and be independent in our own right. This was now more urgent and necessary after a confrontation over a petty misunderstanding which I came face to face with the landlord of our unit and made him realise we were not in awe of him. Luckily all was resolved in years to come, and he helped us out on a project.

I was now on my own again after realising that while in hospital this latest woman in my life was not what I wanted, as she was quite young and immature, and this was resulting in friction with the neighbours. I simply put her gear in black bags and put them out on the lawn.

Going topless

It was back to the night club later on, when another humorous incident occurred. I was wearing a denim shirt, with press studs like pearl buttons. As the evening wore on a particular friend of mine took a fancy to the shirt. He kept on so much that when I was going down the stairs I shouted up to him that he could have it. I took it off, rolled it into a ball and threw it up to him.

At about 1.30 am I was walking home, slightly tipsy, with no shirt on, when two policeman came towards me and challenged me. I said I had been playing cards and lost my shirt, to which they smirked and said "On your way". Just another incident I would like to forget, but I had no one to answer to.

Bad dog impression

Later on in the year I was celebrating my birthday during the day, and went home and went to bed with the intention of coming out again later. My girlfriend at that time had a dog who could be snappy. I thought he was at the foot of the bed, so I decided to lean over the side of the bed in the dark and mimic his growling. The dog jumped up and bit my face, tearing the flesh. Blood spurted out, and I struggled to the bathroom to see that part of my nose was hanging off.

I didn't let that deter me from going to my local later as planned, but it frightened a lot of people when they saw me with loose flesh around my nose!

My brother, after some persuasion took me to hospital, where I had four injections and was stitched up. Drink was partially to blame for another stressful moment.

I was now on my own again.

1991 headlines

US Marines killed at Al Khaiji,
Iraqi troops flee Kuwait

Jubilation follows Gulf War ceasefire

Birmingham Six freed after 16 years

Bomb kills India's former leader Rajiv Gandhi

Bank of Credit and Commerce International
collapses, costing taxpayers millions

Bush opens up historic Middle East peace conference

Publisher Robert Maxwell dies at sea

John McCarthy and church envoy Terry Waite
freed in Beirut.

The music that seems apt for the time is *Dizzy, Any
Dream Will Do, Should I Stay or Should I Go, The One And
Only, Everything I Do I Do It For You, The Shoop Shoop
Song, The Fly.*

.

1992

This was an eventful and quite a traumatic year. We moved to our own premises in a more secluded spot behind a garage with access to the main road. It seemed to be what we had always hoped for, though we had to be more considerate to neighbours close by.

On one occasion in the early days a lorry loaded with large beams backed into the yard badly loaded and the steel came crashing down with a horrendous noise, propelling the neighbours out of their deckchairs.

The only sad thing that hovered over us at this point was that Norman, our main customer from the early days, was fading in a nursing home from cancer. Up to his last days he still had some details for us to produce some metalwork that he required. He died that summer, but we carried out his wishes. He had been without doubt a beacon in our lives. It was he who had got us involved with the Beaujolais Day, and we decided in his memory we would continue to celebrate it for as long as it was held.

Living where I was was OK except that we knew we had to get away at lunchtime and have some peace with a cooked meal. This we always did, and it gave us more energy to last the afternoon. This was heavy work, but travelling three miles each way didn't give me a lot of time as we were quite disciplined. We also had to set an example.

This would be the last time I would get involved in another relationship. It's easy to look back in hindsight and see your mistakes, but this lady seemed nearer my age. After I had helped her with her debts and given her a car for her to go to work, she decided to cross me, so eventually she had to go. I won't elaborate on her exit. But in some ways it was a blessing, because she was quite demanding. I would say there were nymphomaniac traits. She often became depressed, and that I didn't need. I was trying to climb out of that problem.

Taxi across the road

A quite humorous thing happened one night in a nearby town when my mate and I, both quite well oiled, got into a taxi and named the next pub we required, the driver pointed out to us that it was just across the road, to which we replied "Just drive round a little to make it more interesting". When I got home that evening I accidentally shut my right thumb in the door as the driver took off. I was running for dear life until he realised. Yet again drink was partially to blame.

Some of the events of that year

UN threatens Libya with sanctions

Fergie and Prince Andrew split

Controversial Diana book published

IRA murders informers

David Mellor resigns over sex scandal

Thousands or miners to lose their jobs

Church of England votes for women priests,

Queen to start paying tax

Blaze rages in Windsor Castle

Queen's Christmas message leaked.

Songs of the year included *Please Don't Go, Stay, I Will Always Love You, Would I Lie to You, Goodnight Girl, End of the Road, Rhythm Is A Dancer* and *Ain't No Doubt.*

1993

From now on I wanted peace of mind, so it was going to be the dog and me. I did have one final clandestine fling which I will keep under wraps. A special friend of mine and I used to go out regularly on Sunday night, and we went on to share several holidays over the next few years. We also had some great days out at some race meetings.

After settling down to our own environment we were getting to the stage where we could get the jobs we were suited to, especially financially. Another firm on a bigger scale started to take some interest in us and eventually gave us some work, but the real onslaught of work was to follow in the latter part of the nineties.

On weekends when I had my son things were getting easier to handle except that my hand was always in my pocket. But then I wasn't exactly skint, and there was always the odd cash job. The neighbour seemed more content with my new existence, as I was nearly always out. The taxi firms thought I was hyperactive and had a job to keep pace with me. I suppose my attitude as usual was to work hard and play hard as long as I was living alone.

Lager to go

One evening in the pub I was late getting served and my taxi pulled up outside. The landlord said jokingly "Take the pint with you", so I did. When we arrived in the next town a row of people were sitting on a wall outside enjoying the evening sun. When they saw me getting out the taxi with a pint of lager in my hand, they almost choked. They could see I took my drinking seriously!

Around this time I was involved in trying to learn the guitar with a friend from a nearby town. We would meet every Thursday in the studio - he was pretty good. I just had to get my own back after the tuition on the pool table at the local club. I did manage to play guitar a little, but to be honest it was very hard. I was more inquisitive about learning to read music.

We had some great laughs over the next three or four years. He was well respected in town as a good musician, but sadly we lost him to cancer a few years ago.

Headlines of the year

US and Russia agree to halve numbers
of nuclear warheads

World Trade Centre bomb terrorises New York

Two boys charged with murder of
toddler Jamie Bulger

IRA bomb devastates City of London

Green light for Manchester Olympics

Philip Lawrence murder suspects freed

Communist riot in Moscow

Michael Jackson accused of child abuse

Princess Diana sues over gym photos

Secret meetings with IRA revealed

Popular songs at this time included, Relight My Fire, Young at Heart, I'd Do Anything For love, All That She Wants, Oh Caroline.

1994

Over the next 10 years the contracts we took on seemed a lot larger, which entailed more administration and planning. Things were a little quieter when we befriended someone who was to acquire some work for us, but all was to turn sour as the person involved was busy setting up his own rival business, so of course we soon aborted that liaison. We were very organised and as my partner said to me one day when I was working in the rain (on contracts for our main customer), if I could keep the momentum with customers' jobs he would oversee the internal jobs etc. It was more convenient to operate on the large contracts outside due to room, and I usually operated on these as they were expensive. I always thought if I got it wrong when marking it out so be it, but I was happy doing what I had always done.

In my leisure time I eventually went to Zante that year with my Sunday night drinking mate, and the heat was tremendous.

My son was now 12 years old now and was taking an interest in music, so we went see Meat Loaf. His other interest was martial arts. Thinking it would be good for him I took him to sports centres and enrolled him into a class, only to find myself being persuaded to participate. Six months later I was still doing it, but my son had lost interest.

Short taxi trip

One night we met in a pub to go to a skittle match at a pub up the road about 300m away, and unknown to my fellow skittlers I ordered a taxi because it had started raining. When it was time to go they were stunned. I said it was cheaper than getting wet and paying out for a fiver's worth of Anadin!

Getting tanked

On Beaujolais Day we all went to the local wine do at our pub, as we had been doing for years. We shut the workshop up and drank and ate for the rest of the day. The next morning I decided to knock the pub up for six pints of Guinness, and it was about 10 am. Next door there was a garage with people queuing up for fuel, and they were staring at me with this tray of drinks. I got round to the lads and we all sat on the steel and had a hair of the dog. Then a rep pulled up by the gates. He came in looking bewildered and we said to him, "Can't you see this is our break time?"

Popular songs included *Things Can Only Get Better, Dream, Everything Changes, Without You, The Real Thing, Twist and Shout, Saturday Night* and *Stay Another Day.*

1995

A couple of events occurred while I had Layla, my old English Sheepdog. I had temporarily put her on the roof of the office while our main customer came to us to discuss drawings, when all of a sudden urine began to drip from the ceiling on to the drawing. Luckily he had a sense of humour.

Layla and the takeaway

I decided to go out to the pub with Layla, and a few pints later I felt hungry and walked into the Indian restaurant with Layla. She put her front paws upon the counter, and all hell let loose. There were Indians coming from all angles, and I felt like General Custer at his Last Stand. They went ballistic, but I did get my takeaway.

It was a quiet year. My mate and I went to Tenerife for a holiday, and I was playing skittles in the men's league. I did achieve two certificates in the martial arts, which took place in two separate sports centres in front of a lot of people, so I was rather pleased I held my nerve. The music meetings continued, with hope that I might break the ice with the piece *Apache*.

At work it was mainly the five of us with a painter and sometimes some casual labour, but we were a formidable group, and the steel suppliers told us we could turn over more tonnage per man than most. Roll on the Christmas box.

Headlines of the year

Massive earthquake hits Los Angeles

Fred West charged with murders as
body count mounts

Massacre in Rwanda

Ayrton Senna killed at Italian Grand Prix

Camelot wins race for lottery contract

Labour chooses Tony Blair

Israel and Jordan make peace

Cult members die in mass suicide

Russian troops storm into Chechnya.

Killer Ronnie Kray dies

Many die in Oklahoma bombing

Major wins Conservative leadership

Serbs force Muslims out of Srebrenica

OJ Simpson acquitted of killing wife

Ecstasy puts party girl in a coma

Diana admits adultery in TV interview

Hit music of the time included *I believe, Bombastic, Think Twice, Cotton Eyed Joe, Back for Good, Don't Stop, Earth Song.*

1996

This year I obtained one more martial art certificate, but one frosty day I bent over and jerked a large piece of steel out of the way of a lorry reversing in, which resulted in me getting a hernia. I suppose after 16 years of shifting steel I did OK really in the injuries department, but we were rated high risk by insurance companies.

I went for an operation privately and was home the next day. By evening I was out in the local club playing pool. Pretty crazy when I evaluate it now. I could have stayed away from work, and my partner tried to persuade me to take a few days off. With a hernia operation it hurts to cough or laugh.

Coming home late one night a week or so later I realised I had left my keys indoors. The taxi driver looked on in shock as I scaled the door on the side of the house, then got up on the garage roof and did a Spiderman round to the bedroom window. As I heaved myself into the aperture I got stuck with my rear on view for the whole of cul de sac to see. Layla was pleased to see me, but I was stuck there for at least 10 minutes. The taxi driver to this day can't forget this occurrence. She said she would put it in her memoirs.

Mind your own business

My opinionated and old-fashioned neighbours were retired and spent most of the time in the garden. He was in awe of his wife, scared of her even. One particularly hot day I was loading an Artic 40 lorry with steel and drove home to cook my dinner. As I approached my driveway he was up a ladder cleaning the gutter and he was holding the ladder steady as I got out the car with my shirt stuck to my back. She said "My husband's not being lazy like you, he's up there cleaning the guttering." I saw red and said "Why don't you mind your own bloody business?" She said she had never been so insulted in all her life, and I told her she obviously didn't get around much.

News stories of the year

US peacekeepers power into Bosnia

France halts nuclear testing

First GM food goes on sale in the UK

Bomb blast destroys London bus

Children massacred at
Dunblane school – handguns banned

Girl survives murder of mother and sister

Afghan forces rocked as Kabul falls

Hijacked jet crashes into the sea.

Music of the time included *Don't Look Back in Anger, Ooh Ahh Just a Little Bit, Ready or Not, Killing Me Softly, Wannabe, Words, I Feel For You, Breath, Say You'd be There, Three Lions, How Deep is Your Love.*

1997

We were now pretty settled at our premises and were busy dealing with an old friend for whom we had done structural building work. He had his own company and was using us as a supplier, mainly for cladding parts, basically miscellaneous quantities of plates, angles etc. It was hard going at times because of the deadlines we had to meet with all the customers busy at once. My partner and I would plan the order for the steel to come in. Our own efficiency in not letting anyone down led to more demand and we were sometimes our own worst enemy. It seemed that the older we got the harder we worked, and we started to work the next six months just to keep pace with the tax bill. I can't complain in some ways because I was able to move into the premises I am in today, tucked up on the outskirts of town.

One day the police called and said I had been reported for resembling a person wanted for a murder down in Plymouth. I explained that I wished I had time to go to Plymouth but I was always nailed to work. They said they were thinking of arresting me but came back later to say it was a mistake. I still wonder if this was a wind up.

Some news events

Princess Diana dies in Paris car crash

Gianni Versace murdered on doorstep

Dolly the sheep is cloned

Tiger Woods wins masters at 21

Gordon Brown sets Bank of England free

IRA declares ceasefire

Mother Teresa dies

Angry truckmen blockade French ports

Michael Hutchence found dead in hotel

Great Train Robber Biggs escapes extradition again.

The music at the time included *D'you Know What I mean, I Believe I Can Fly, Ain't Nobody, Candle in the Wind 1997, Perfect Day, I'll be missing you, You're Not Alone, Men in Black.*

1998

Between 1997 and 1999 nothing of significance happened with the business. We were engrossed in work to complete the Millennium order and rarely had a day away from work.

Some of the events of the year

Northern Ireland peace deal reached

Dozens die in Omagh bombing

Clinton admits Lewinsky affair

Thousands flee fighting in Kosovo

Real IRA announces ceasefire

Iraq climbdown averts air strikes

Queen's speech spells end for peers

World fury at Pakistan's nuclear tests

Hundreds die in Swiss air crash.

The music from 1998 included *Never Ever, My Heart Will Go On, All That I Need, Viva Forever, No Matter What, Millennium, I Want You Back To You I Belong.*

1999

Over the next two years I went to night school, studied Spanish and obtained my level two proficiency test with 96%, going on to do another year. The next two years I felt the work and pace we had to go was taking its toll on us, but we both had escape valves. I liked the odd race meeting and my partner had afternoons playing golf.

I wanted to be in two places at once. My partner was tied up more and more with paperwork and I felt at times out of touch because I was concentrating on large steel contracts which had to be correct because of the costs involved. As long as I prepared the steel to the drawings I felt content, and there always a man we had who usually was involved with other specialist jobs who could assist when we could spare him.

When I was in the office, I always felt my place was out among the lads working with them as an example and for any queries they might have, but I suppose it was the Irish navvy in me.

I personally was happy as long as those lads were. I always said from the early days that you are only as good as the blokes you employ, as one bad apple can cause a problem. We helped them as much as we could. After all, we relied on each other.

At this time took massive orders for the Millennium Stadium.

On the leisure front, we went to some of the local Harvest Homes, but the Beaujolais days were fading out. Harvest time was generally like a fair with marquees and usually a band.

News events

Olympic officials face bribery charges

Dozens hurt by Soho nail bomb

Turkey hit by huge earthquake

Men in custody after burglary and shooting

Death toll rising in Paddington rail crash

UK pressure to celebrate Millennium

Putin takes over in Russia as Yeltsin resigns.

The music from 1999 included *Heartbeat, When the Going Gets Tough, You Needed Me, Bring it All Back, Boom Boom Bang Boom, If I Let You Go, Mamba No 5, She's the One, I Have a Dream.*

2000

We met all the demands for production associated with the Millennium Stadium. Most of the time someone was working in the evenings, and we even had a bloke who came to help us who was once the steward from the local club. We were careful who we had as it's better the devil you know.

My partner was generally good at organising steel parts and quantity jobs, and his experience in the past had stood him in good stead. As he said a few times, he felt like a juggler trying to keep customers happy on deliveries. It was so busy that we promised the staff that if they stood by us and maintained the momentum we would pay for a holiday for all to Tenerife. As we achieved the goal we did just that and eight of us flew there. We had a week to remember.

Lasered

In my late forties I was getting short-sighted. When I was burning steel I had to wear glasses and goggles as well, which became uncomfortable and the goggles would mist up. After seeing the advert for Optimal I applied to have it done. The day arrived for me to go to

Bristol with my brother-in-law for the procedure. When I arrived I filled in the necessary forms and they said they would do one eye at a time - one today, the other at a later date in case of any problems.

They were shocked when I said I didn't want to keep coming back up and down to Bristol and wanted them to do both eyes today. It was done, with the surgeon shaking his head in disbelief. I lay back in the chair and coloured lotion was put in both eyes and laser applied. It all seemed to be over in five or six minutes. I was led out with my eyes covered and a handful of painkillers.

As I lived on my own my sister and brother-in-law came home and sat me up in the chair with a glass of lager and some painkillers, then set off to go out for the evening. As the night wore on the pain began to grow. Fumbling for the tablets, I knocked them off the table, but I couldn't see a thing and by now the pain was excruciating. If I could have found a knife I would have ended it all. I couldn't even use the phone. Then all of a sudden they came back to do a spot check on me, thank heavens. Trust me to go the whole hog.

Events of the year

World celebrates new millennium

Life for serial killer Harold Shipman

Ford quits Dagenham after 70 years

Sarah Payne's body found

Rescuers race to save stricken Russian submarine

Bush pips Gore to the post in presidential election

Four dead in Hatfield rail crash

Freezing Britain grinds to a halt

Steve Redgrave wins fifth Olympic gold.

Popular songs that year included: *You See the Trouble With Me, Don't Give Up, Against All Odds, Life is a Roller Coaster, Bag it up, Go Let it Out, Day and Night, Take on Me.*

2001

I was now on the eve of my 50ᵗʰ birthday. We had another busy year, but not too much to report. A couple more contracts went through that we didn't get paid for, but we half knew this would happen. The trouble is if you're quieter the temptation is there and you don't have a crystal ball. On reflection I sometimes wondered if we might have over done the appreciation for the staff with holidays etc, but I am so glad we did as we always have the memories of going out together, not just work. We didn't have money to burn, but it might have looked that way.

My younger brother came back to live locally and soon got involved with skittles and going to see local cricket. It was during this year I scored a 100 pins with 7 to start and followed with 6 spares (no strikes), 7.14.14.15.17.17.16 = 100, for the second time.

We would occasionally book a mini bus and go to the resort of Brean six miles away and have a little tour of the pubs, which was always easy going and fun.

Some of the events of that year

Terrorists destroy World Trade Centre in New York with the loss of 3000 lives; War on Terror begins.

10 die in Selby rail crash

Foot and mouth disease strikes UK

Ex Yugoslav leader Milosevic arrested after siege

Race violence erupts in Burnley

In the charts were *Gotta Get Through This, Another Chance, Let's Dance, Have you ever, Can't Get You Out Of My Head, It's Raining Men, Pure and Simple, The Way To Your Love.*

2002

This is when I came close to my past as it approaches my 50th year, but I will skim over 2003-2004 to reach a couple of humorous events in 2005. This was the last year when I would say I was fit mentally and physically, as problems were developing. Up to this point I could still walk along with an RSJ girder carry 150kg and do most physical tasks. Work was quite busy, especially with the large steel contracts which I got satisfaction in producing, but quite wearing. As long as my partner was happy I was generally OK. We couldn't let our personal lives cast a shadow over the business.

Later on this year we went to the races as a day out on my birthday. I can recall one of our friends asking for a tip. I duly obliged. I thought he had £10 on it but he had put £4000 on it at 11/4. No wonder he picked me up off my feet when it won.

Some of the events that year

Celebrations as euro hits the streets

UK declared free of foot and mouth

Hindus die in train fire

Queen Mother dies at 101

Brothers cleared of Damilola Taylor murder

Dozens killed in Bali nightclub explosion

Diana Ross arrested for drink driving

Riots force missionary workers out of Nigeria.

Hit music at this time included *Anything is Possible, More Than a Woman, The Tide is High, World of Our Own, If Tomorrow Never Comes, If You're Not The One, Sound of the Underground, Love Yourself* and *Round Round.*

2003

In February/March of this year I developed a pain in my back which began to drag my health down over the next few years. To make things more traumatic, my Old English sheepdog Layla was fading. It got to the stage where I would spend most of the weekends at home with two chairs put together and me stretched out on them. And at work I couldn't turn the steel over. I needed assistance, and the constant pain was grinding me down. The doctor and the physio couldn't do much to alleviate my situation.

I felt a horrible depression coming on, so I eventually went private and out of my own pocket paid £800 to get an answer. I was told I had to see a specialist physiotherapist or have an operation. This was quite risky as it involved the spine, so I embarked on physio treatment. The basic problem was a compounded disc and trapped sciatic nerves. The pain sometimes made me feel sick and of course now work had become a challenge to me as this was pain was draining me. I knew I had to rebuild my back with careful exercise.

In the news

Saddam regime topples – Saddam captured
in underground lair

Comedian Bob Hope dies at 100

Britain swelters in record heat

Johnny Cash dies

End of an era for Concorde

England win Rugby World Cup

Ian Huntley guilty of Soham child murders

Libya gives up chemical weapons.

Popular music included *Bring me Back to Life, Never Gonna Leave Your Side, Are You Ready For Love, Mandy, Changes.*

2004

Coming into this year I finally lost my old dog Layla after a battle to keep her going over the last 12 months. I was persuaded to replace her with a Jack Russell, which was the best decision I made.

Throughout this year the pain was wearing me down and lowering my resistance. If I hadn't been working for myself I would probably have been off work. My partner was doing his best to handle the situation but it must have been very frustrating at times.

Work became an ordeal, and it came to the stage when I was glad to get home and lie down.

In the news

Serial killer Harold Shipman found hanged

US transfers power back to Iraq

Second gold for athlete Kelly Holmes

George Bush wins second term

Yasser Arafat dies dead

Thousands die in Asian tsunami

Russian School siege ends in violence.

We were listening to *Take Me to the Clouds, Dry Your Eyes, With a Little Help From My Friends (yet another version), Obviously Real To Me, I'll Stand By You.*

2005

I had an appointment at the local medical centre one dark wet miserable Wednesday evening. I sat there waiting until the receptionist went out of the door and I was suddenly in the dark. It now dawned on me that I was alone, so I went up the corridor checking. When I came back I saw a taxi outside, but I could not open the door as it was locked. I went back down the corridor scouting about when all of a sudden a doctor came in. He asked me what I was doing there and I said I was hoping to see a doctor. In the end I got a lift home with a friend.

Rear entry

This is the term I used to describe the medical procedure I now had to undergo, a delicate subject to say the least. After years of heavy lifting and not the best sort of diet I was blessed with piles. I eventually plucked up the courage to see the doctor and was sent to a local hospital to have it sorted, I was told to get up on the table and put myself on my hands and knees, head down, hands more or less level with my forehead, with my pants down, my rear poking up ready for tackling.

I noticed peopled coming in and out of the door and asked the nurse to pull the screens round. She wondered why I was agitated and I said everyone could be watching me, even the tea lady. After about five minutes of having a gadget like a bellows operated on me it occurred to me that it was like a Kwik Fit operator doing up a wheelnut.

When all was done, the surgeon asked how I was and I said I was going to put it all behind me now. I proceeded to walk to the toilets with legs apart like a gunfighter. I eventually sat in my sister's car as stiff as a plank.

You could say that this brings the curtains down. On reflection I suppose "Health is Wealth" but sometimes wealth can buy health. If you have your health then most things seem possible. You hope that good times outweigh the bad, and you will one day look back and laugh.

News events of the year

Ellen MacArthur sails into record books

Charles and Camilla to marry

Ban on hunting comes into force

Syrian troops leave Lebanon

Blair secures historic third term

G8 Leaders agree €50 billion aid boost

England wins the Ashes

Bomb rips through Bali restaurant

Pubs open 24 hours a day

David Cameron is new Tory Leader

Massive fire at Buncefield oil depot.

Songs that year included *Sometimes You Can't Make It On Your Own, Lonely, Is This The Way to Amarillo, You're Beautiful, Push the Button, I bet You Look Good on the Dance Floor, Hung Up, That's My Goal.*

Throughout the latter part of 2005 until I finished I was taking more time off. I couldn't understand why everything was a challenge, and felt as though the back problem had worn me down. For once in my life I had to be giving in. Eventually the problem was diagnosed as neurological. I knew I couldn't contribute fairly to the business in the future, so I retired.

I wasn't really well enough to handle the financial affairs relating to the business, this was left to my partner and our accountants. I trusted them as they had always treated me fairly.

2007

After finishing work in 2007 I was struggling to adjust to the medication and the drastic change in my life, going from working among seven or eight men with steel deliveries, phones ringing, customers coming in to discuss jobs. After all the hustle and bustle I was living in a room of silence.

The most important thing was not to suffer from depression. After about eight or nine months I decided to chance buying a racehorse. I had budgeted for three or four years.

I had followed racing since I was eight years old. As I said earlier in this book, concentrating on the racing page eased my breathing problems because I was relaxed. As I got into my teens I would write my bets out and my father or grandad would put them on. During the summer evenings I used to go gardening in the village, then walk up to my grandad's house. He would sit in the shed at the bottom of the garden listening to the night results, drinking cider and eating cheese and bread.

All through the sixties I followed the racing pages, and even in the seventies when I had a job in the sales office I was helping out Saturdays in the local betting office. Luckily I had an outside line, and when I occasionally put a bet on an important race I would get the bookies to put the phone next to the tannoy system so I could hear the race in the office.

Later on I went to quite a few race meetings. Eventually I went ahead and met a trainer locally and asked him to set about purchasing a horse for me over the jumps. I eventually went 50-50 with its current half owner. To our dismay the horse had to have a sinus operation, but she recovered. She ran second in her first race at 66/1 with some minor placing, but she got beaten at Chepstow, so she was a year off being ready at least.

In the meanwhile she had a foal, but she was now getting prepared to race this year. Eventually, at the end of 2011 she was ready to race, but suddenly she had a hairline fracture. As far as I was concerned this was the end, as we had had so much bad luck. Enough was enough.

I found a home for her - the trainer and his wife said they would have her. They said that if they got her right they would race her in our names to try and give us back something, as we had been so patient and so unlucky.

She ran at Taunton and had to be pulled up, but the dream came true when she ran at Fontwell and won at 20/1 by 45 lengths! She followed up on Boxing Day at Fontwell with another win at 6/4, by 21 lengths.

On a more poignant note, my brother and brother-in-law came to watch her, but they never lived long enough to see her win. My brother was taken from us with motor neurone disease and my brother-in-law with heart complications. It felt as though they were watching.

Unfortunately it was a sad ending for the horse too. Following her victory at Fontwell Park, she was injured on a later visit and had to be put down. However she left us with a three-year-old colt (yet to be named) which we are hoping will run on the flat in the future.

4102863R00092

Printed in Great Britain
by Amazon.co.uk, Ltd.,
Marston Gate.